BRICK FLICKS

BRICK FLICKS

A COMPREHENSIVE GUIDE TO MAKING YOUR OWN
STOP-MOTION LEGO® MOVIES

SARAH HERMAN

Skyhorse Publishing

Skyhorse Publishing books may be purchased in bulk at special discounts for sales promotion, corporate gifts, fund-raising, or educational purposes. Special editions can also be created to specifications. For details, contact the Special Sales Department, Skyhorse Publishing, 307 West 36th Street, 11th Floor, New York, NY 10018 or info@skyhorsepublishing.com.

Skyhorse® and Skyhorse Publishing® are registered trademarks of Skyhorse Publishing, Inc.®, a Delaware corporation.

Visit our website at www.skyhorsepublishing.com.

10 9 8 7 6 5 4 3 2 1

Library of Congress Cataloging-in-Publication Data is available on file.

Cover design by Paul Hollingsworth and Brian Peterson
Cover photo credit by Paul Hollingsworth

Print ISBN: 978-1-62914-649-2
Ebook ISBN: 978-1-62914-888-5

Printed in China

CONTENTS

AUTHOR'S NOTE

The term "brick-film" or "brickfilm" is believed to have been coined by Jason Rowoldt, who founded the website Brickfilms.com in 2000—the first popular Internet destination for the hobby. This book is not affiliated with or endorsed by Brickfilms.com and the terms "brick-film," "brick-filmer," and "brick-filmmaking" are merely used colloquially to refer to LEGO stop-motion animation, as is common in the community.

The advice in this book has been garnered from eighteen filmmakers and animators who make brick-films, some amateurs and some professionals. While it aims to cover all that you'll need to know to get started, it's by no means a definitive user guide for the dozens of computer programs you may choose to use to make your movies. Please refer to the resources section at the back of the book for useful web links and further reading suggestions.

Paul Hollingsworth produced much of the photography in this book. Paul is a father, film editor, and fan of all things LEGO. Playing with LEGO as a child eventually led Paul to the sunny hills of Hollywood where he now works as one of the animators for the web series *LEGO Mixels*. He also creates stunning stop-motion animations with Digital Wizards—a creative team of artists who together have produced more than twenty-five stop-motion animations, winning prizes at BrickCon, BrickFest, and a number of other contests. All their animations can be found at www.DigitalWizards.tv.

INTRODUCTION

INTRODUCTION

Bricks, camera, action! Welcome to the wonderful world of stop-motion animation, with LEGO! This is the hobby that brings the backlot to your basement and puts you in the director's chair. Who needs exotic locations, big-name stars, or million-dollar budgets when you can build and shoot any scene imaginable with a box of bricks and some basic photography equipment? Whether you're filming a space battle in a galaxy far, far away, looking to make your very own music video, or recreating classic cinema in glorious plastic, it's all possible with LEGO stop-motion.

Behind the scenes of one of the earliest LEGO stop-motion films, *The Magic Portal* by Lindsay Fleay.
© Lindsay Fleay

Starting at the very beginning is always sensible, so I've included a brief history of LEGO on film to launch you into the hobby. It's fascinating to see the development of the medium, both with official projects from the LEGO Group and amateur releases. Drawing inspiration from those who have impressed audiences before you is a great way to kick-start any new project, so you'll find lots of references to online materials and videos (with details at the back of the book).

There are those who might like to take a risk and experiment without understanding the principles of stop-motion, and the most efficient way to do things, but if you're going to be spending time, and possibly money, on setting yourself up to make your own LEGO films, then it makes good sense to know what you're getting into first. If you're reading this book, chances are you want guidance and advice on essential equipment, cameras, and required software features—you will find all of this and more in chapter three.

Chapter four takes an in-depth look at how lighting can be used to increase your audience's appreciation of your movies—communicating mood, time of day, and enhancing narrative, while chapter five advises you on how to select an appropriate studio space, how to set it up, and prepare to film your first project. While it might seem easier to ignore these early steps, get your camera out, and just start shooting, you'll be glad you took the time to prepare properly. Something that's seemingly unimportant, like the type of surface you have chosen to build your set on, could have a dramatic effect on the quality of your finished film, as you will soon discover.

Chapter six is where you'll learn the basics of stop-motion animation and how those underpinning principles can be applied to animating with minifigures, and other LEGO stop-motion projects. What you'll soon come to understand is that whether you're making a minifigure fly through the air or turning a sloped brick into a moving blob, the same important rules need to be adhered to for the audience to believe what they're seeing is actually moving by itself.

As with most things, you will learn best by doing. While chapter seven looks more closely at filmmaking and storytelling, and the steps you can take to develop a project *before* you start shooting, that doesn't mean you have to wait until you have a finessed script, storyboard, and shooting schedule to start practicing your stop-motion skills. Throughout the book you will notice small "Activity" icons that indicate an ideal place to put the book down and have a go yourself. They look like this: 📷. These are suggestions for how you can put what you've just read into practice, but by no means feel restricted by them. If you want to try out something different, go ahead, but be sure to apply as much advice as you have absorbed at each stage.

For some, shooting and simple editing may suffice, but this guide would be incomplete without the offerings of chapter eight, where we explore some of the myriad options for finishing your film professionally. There are software recommendations, a guide to your postproduction workflow, and suggestions for editing, sound, and visual effects. As with your stop-motion skills, time spent practicing postproduction techniques will soon become apparent both in the efficiency with which you can complete a production and the quality of the finish, so it's worth pushing yourself outside of your comfort zone to achieve this.

Finally, there is an entire chapter dedicated to sharing your hobby and films with the world, with ideas on how to upload, present, and promote your movies, as well as a look at the community of LEGO stop-motion films. The Internet has seen an explosion of brick-film hobbyists in recent years, and for those who animate solo, the online community offers a place to share ideas, ask for help, and see what other people are up to.

Great advice comes from a wealth of experience, and all the expertise in this book has been derived from those in the know. Many of the stop-motion tutorials have been quarried from the mind of professional animator Tony Mines of Spite

Your Face Productions. Between 1999 and 2004, he produced eight stop-motion LEGO animations, including five for the LEGO Group. These include the first original stop-motion LEGO film online, the first fully stop-motion LEGO licensed film online, and the first original licensed Star Wars animation of the twenty-first century. Tony's films are widely recognized in the brick-film community as being a primary influence and inspiration for what is now a popular global hobby. Needless to say, you're in good hands.

In addition to Tony's advice, seventeen other filmmakers have contributed their tips and tricks for producing stop-motion films with LEGO, including Oscar-winner Michel Gondry, *Edward and Friends* director Martin Pullen, *The Magic Portal* director Lindsay Fleay, and the animators behind some of the most popular LEGO films

© Paul Hollingsworth

on YouTube. Throughout the book you'll also find exclusive interviews with these creative individuals, where they discuss their most successful projects, problems they've faced, and solutions they've discovered.

Your LEGO stop-motion animations can be as simple or as complex as you want them to be. From thirty-second shorts to epic feature films filled with effects that wouldn't be out of place in your local multiplex, the brick-filming pantheon has it all. The limits are the LEGO bricks you film and the imagination you harness. So what are you waiting for filmmakers? It's time to dust off your LEGO sets, position your camera, and prepare to make some movie magic of your own.

1

BRICKS ON FILM

LEGO IN MOTION—A BRIEF HISTORY

The debut of 2014's hugely successful *The LEGO Movie* might be the first time many people made the connection between LEGO and the big screen, or any screen for that matter. While the CGI sensation might be the Danish brand's first taste of box office victory, it's not the first time LEGO toys have found themselves included in a feature film or been the subject of an animated television series. Take a trip down memory lane with this potted history of LEGO's animated career.

Advertising

Some of the earliest appearances of LEGO minifigures and their brick-built surroundings can be found in the same place as most other popular children's toys—television advertising. LEGO fans of most generations will recall TV commercials from their childhoods. European children of the 1950s might remember the first ever LEGO TV commercial featuring the slogan *Wir bauen eine stadt*—German for "We build a city." The short film features a family settling down to build an entire city from the original town plan theme and its 700 series gift boxes of red and white

bricks. The video features a small amount of stop-motion at the end as the bricks arrange themselves to create the company logo.

In the 1970s and into the early 1980s, the majority of TV commercials focused on the versatility of LEGO toys—"It's a new toy every day" was one such accompanying slogan and "Toys that build imagination" was another. The popular British comedian Tommy Cooper voiced an advertisement that saw real LEGO bricks morphing from tiny mice into giant dogs, fire engines, and submarine-eating kippers. These ads incorporated LEGO stop-motion to speed up the construction process, showing children that the only real limits to building were their imaginations and time (oh, and the size of their LEGO collection). This was before the 1978 introduction of the LEGO minifigure, which completely transformed the toy manufacturer's approach. Suddenly, there were characters populating the imaginative worlds children were building, and these characters soon became the focus of advertising campaigns.

The late 1980s and 1990s saw a radical shift toward action-based commercials, which featured children playing with the toys accompanied by dramatic music and a character-themed story line. Often the child in question was referred to as Zack the LEGO Maniac. Zack, wearing shades and a LEGO jacket, had his own theme song and was the company's attempt to inject a sense of "cool" into its new space themed lines.

Advance, an independent creative communication agency based in Denmark, has worked with LEGO on commercial animations for over thirty years. Its archives consist of some of the most memorable 1990s LEGO commercials for product lines including: Castle, Adventurers, Bellville, ZNAP, Islanders, and DUPLO. Some of the methods employed by Advance (and others) in the past, where LEGO toys are "magically" constructed, would not be allowed under more recent

advertising standards, which must show the toy being physically built or maneuvered if it cannot move on its own in actuality (a LEGO helicopter flying, for example). This has meant that there is relatively little stop-motion animation in LEGO advertising and the commercials largely featured the LEGO being filmed in situ with children's hands maneuvering the pieces to create action. In some cases, fake hands were used to try and get a shot that would be considered suitable.

While some of the more recent commercials have included 2D or CGI animation to help dramatize the toy, these commercials indicate how much can be achieved with LEGO as a cinematic subject without the use of stop-motion or other forms of animation. Clever cuts, angles, and

Edward the Elephant in the largely unseen 1980s TV show *Edward and Friends*.
© Martin Pullen. Used with permission of the LEGO Group.

practical shots, such as pushing a car to make it move, can be time-saving and equally effective.

Edward and Friends

Made in the late 1980s in the United Kingdom, *Edward and Friends* was the first TV program produced by LEGO. Initially pitched to the BBC, LEGO had intended for the series to feature their range of Fabuland toys using stop-motion animation. Fabuland appeared on shelves in 1979, and targeted the transitional age group of children moving from DUPLO's basic building blocks to more versatile LEGO sets and minifigures. The sets incorporated LEGO bricks, and larger pre-built LEGO compatible parts, but crucially featured Fabuland's anthropomorphic inhabitants—minifigure-style animal critters with larger bodies. Fabuland sold well throughout the 1980s, until 1989 when the last sets were released.

Laws prohibiting the use of existing toy products in television programming encouraged the show's developers to create clay models based on the line's characters, and to call the show *Edward and Friends*, referring to the central character of Edward the Elephant rather than pushing the Fabuland brand. Two seasons of the show were made, twenty-six episodes in total. Unfortunately, the program was not picked up by any British broadcasters, although it did find a home on Canadian TV and VHS videos. See page 6 for an interview with one of the show's directors, Martin Pullen.

BRICKS ON FILM

Martin Pullen animated and directed for the 1987 animated series *Edward and Friends* made by British production company FilmFair for LEGO. He has also worked on the popular animated series *Fifi and the Flowertots* and *The Koala Brothers.*

How did you become involved as an animator and director on *Edward and Friends*?

I was working at FilmFair directing *Paddington.* When that came to an end, they asked me if I wanted to go and animate on *Edward and Friends*, which was already running and starting to animate. There were some problems—the animation was going really slowly, and the original director was sacked—and the three of us [Martin Pullen, Jo Pullen, and Jeff Newitt] took over directing.

Were you excited to work on the project?

I didn't know that much about it, but I certainly enjoyed it. It was a very nice thing to work on. It was well made; there was a certain quality about it. A lot of stuff that FilmFair

"Each building, piece of parkland, and so on was a section that would lift out if not needed," says Martin Pullen. "The boxes under the set were low, which meant either kneeling on the floor or crouching on the set to animate."
© Martin Pullen. Used with permission of the LEGO Group.

had done up to that point, in comparison on a budget scale per minute, had a lot lower budget, lower production values. *Edward and Friends* was shot on 35mm film, whereas before that things had always been shot on 16mm Bolex, which made the actual physical quality of the end production a lot higher. There was a lot more crew involved and the puppets were very well made so you could do some decent animations with them.

Why was the budget a lot higher for this production?

There are two ways of making a program. One is that it's financed by the production company, so FilmFair financed *The Wombles* and *Paddington*, for example, whereas this

was financed by LEGO so FilmFair was merely a production company being paid to make the program.

What was the set like?

It was made like an enormous jigsaw puzzle so there were loads and loads of pieces, so you put whatever pieces together that you needed to shoot from different angles. That was quite time-consuming. Also, not that it ever really worked, there was a huge motion-control rig hanging from the ceiling that was being built. I think that cost several thousand pounds to build, so you could do sweeping shots across the studio and things like that. At that point, I certainly hadn't filmed anything with a motion-control setup before.

"There was a separate shooting area for interiors," says Martin. "You can see where pins are pushed in the feet to stop the puppets falling over. We had colored cardboard to cover the underneath of a foot if it could be seen, which is missing from the mouse on the left in this photo."
© Martin Pullen. Used with permission of the LEGO Group.

How was LEGO involved with the day-to-day running of the show?

Their contingent came over occasionally to see how things were going. When programs were edited together they were sent over to Denmark for them to look at and approve. So I think they had approval of the edit, before all the grading and postproduction. But they weren't in the studio much, but there's not a great reason to be in the studio. It's a slow process. There wasn't all the technology then where you see it as you go along. You would film for three, four, or five days and then the film would be unloaded and sent off to be developed.

Did that result in frames having to be reshot?

It's not very often that things would get reshot, unless there was something really seriously wrong with it. You were shooting blind—you didn't have any assist to see what you were shooting. Nowadays you take your frame, if you don't like it you delete it, move your puppet, and take it again. You had to get it right the first time through your knowledge of how to animate a character.

How was the directing divided up between the three of you?

We didn't divide them up. We were co-directors, in effect. So we'd sit down in a room with the script and bash out a storyboard between the three of us and then we'd go and get it filmed. We didn't say this episode's mine and this is yours. I guess Jeff and myself would animate maybe fifteen to twenty seconds a day between the pair of us. So in a week we'd probably do a minute. We worked on the show for around eighteen months.

Were all the sets and models already built when you started on the show?

It was already created. There were model makers making extra stuff as we went along, as there'd be things that were specific to each episode, but it had already been designed and created before I got involved. The models were very small compared to other ones I'd worked on, but they were well made. I think they were about five inches tall and quite chunky. They had ball and socket joints covered in latex.

Does that make them easier to animate?

They were quite easy to animate. You know how the LEGO figures'

arms don't bend all over the place like a normal puppet would? They made their arms quite straight to keep them in a LEGO style. In the same way the heads would rotate without going all over the place like a normal puppet. They did stand up well because they weren't very tall and the feet were quite sizeable. They didn't have a tendency to fall over too much. We used long pins—the sets were made out of pin board, soft board we used to call it, so you could push them on pins through the feet and into the floor.

What did you enjoy most about working on the show?

I think I enjoyed the fact it was a large production in a huge studio. It was one of the better things that I worked on. I particularly enjoyed the sequences that we did that were about ten or twelve seconds long to link episodes together. They were one-off jokes and I remember the three of us sitting in a room,

throwing ideas about, picking out the best ones. We had a lot of freedom to do what we wanted with those. There was one, which I animated, it was a tightrope between two boxes, and you thought that Edward the Elephant was going to walk this tightrope, so he stepped up onto the box, took a bow, and then when he stepped onto the wire the wire was actually made of rubber so he bounced onto the floor and then just walked along to the other box.

Did you think that the show would be broadcast, and did you think that it was going to be successful?

I never thought it would be broadcast. So it was only ever going to come out on video, which didn't bother me. I was paid to direct programs and that was it, whether they were a success of not. I will always do the best I possibly can within the time available to do it, and hopefully enjoy doing it whether or not people are going to see it. It never really mattered to me.

Did you get to keep any of the puppets or anything from the show?

When we finished we had to box up all the pieces of set, the puppets, and the molds, and everything was shipped off to Denmark. I went over to Billund [Denmark] at a later date for a meeting, and they were all over there. I saw some of the puppets on display.

In this episode, Lionel the Lion, the mayor of Fabuland, had moles in his garden. "The puppets' eyes were made from resin in molds," says Martin. "They would pop out for replacement positions for blinks and looking different ways, making them easy and effective to animate."
© Martin Pullen. Used with permission of the LEGO Group.

LEGO Studios

In 2000 the LEGO Group joined forces with acclaimed director Steven Spielberg to launch a toy line that would add a whole new dimension to LEGO play. LEGO Studios was a partnership that attempted to harness the growing popularity of brick-filmmaking and package it for the brand's target market. The LEGO & Steven Spielberg MovieMaker Set included LEGO bricks and pieces to recreate a dinosaur action scene, along with a minifigure film crew. The LEGO was packaged with a USB camera and editing software co-produced by the company's media arm and Pinnacle Systems. Over the following two years, related sets released under the LEGO Studios banner included a range of classic cinematic scenarios, as well as the Jurassic Park III and first Spider-Man sets, but none of these included the camera and editing software. Despite the growing popularity of LEGO stop-motion, the line ended in 2002, just as the brick-film community started to grow and only three years prior to the launch of YouTube and the online explosion of the hobby. Included on DVDs with the second series of sets was the first LEGO-commissioned animations comprised entirely of stop-motion to illustrate to children what was possible.

The demise of the LEGO Studios line can be attributed in part to the company's timing, and also to the limitations set by the product they produced. In the early 2000s, YouTube still hadn't been founded, and DSLRs were not affordable; this was also a period of financial turmoil for the Danish giant, which announced a record deficit of some $230 million. The brand had lost its way and was fighting tooth and nail to try and keep customers—the main strategy seemed to involve the constant release of new building themes and off-shoot toys, most of which didn't survive. One main criticism of LEGO Studios was the upper frame rate that was set in the software of 15fps, software that was essentially a watered-down version of what it could have been. LEGO underestimated the technological know-how of its audience, and the wider adult appeal of LEGO films.

LEGO films, TV series, and video games

In the decade since the disappearance of the LEGO Studios line, LEGO characters have appeared in over twenty films beginning with 2003's *Bionicle: Mask of Light*—one of the USA's top ten DVD premiere titles of that year. The hugely successful Bionicle line spawned three other DVD releases, all of which were CG animated. The Clutch Powers series, LEGO Star Wars shorts, and Ninjago TV series have all been produced using CG animation—modeling characters on their minifigure relations, albeit with more flexibility and naturalistic facial expressions. This style of animation has also been used in cut scenes of all the LEGO video games from *LEGO Batman* to *LEGO Harry Potter*. The most recent interpretation of LEGO on screen can be seen in *The LEGO Movie*, which started development in 2008 and was released to an overwhelmingly positive reception in 2014. Unlike the earlier, more cartoony approaches to the subject matter, the Warner Bros. Pictures film created a more tangible world, going so far as to recreate the plastic markings and scratches on the surface of the minifigure characters, resulting in a realistic stop-motion-esque finish. At the time of writing there are plans for a Ninjago feature film and a sequel to *The LEGO Movie*, the latter slated for release in 2017.

THE ART OF STOP-MOTION ANIMATION

What is stop-motion animation?

Unlike traditional 2D animation, where a series of incrementally different drawings are photographed and played back quickly to give the illusion of movement, stop-motion animation requires the animator to move real objects or puppets in front of the camera before capturing a still image of the objects in that position. The animator then adjusts the object, often only very slightly, and takes another photograph. This process is repeated to build up seconds of animation, which are compiled to create entire animated feature films. Because of the time-consuming and costly nature of stop-motion versus 2D animation, in the past you were more likely to see the medium in the form of children's television programs and commercials. But with the recent technological development in digital cameras and animation software, and an affinity for the tactile quality of puppetry over 2D cartoons, stop-motion animation has experienced a renaissance over the last decade or so. A number of successful movies have been animated in this way including *The Nightmare Before Christmas, James and the Giant Peach, Chicken Run, Wallace & Gromit: The Curse of the Were-Rabbit, Coraline, Fantastic Mr. Fox,* and *ParaNorman,* to name a few.

What makes stop-motion animation so much fun?

"I love animation because of the way that it brings things to life, things that your brain knows can't be brought to life," said Chris Salt, which is especially true of LEGO stop-motion where these familiar objects appear to be moving. He refers to the way John Lasseter used 3D animation to give two desk lamps character in the 1986 Pixar short *Luxo Jr.* just by making them move in different ways—in the same way legendary animator and cinematic legend Ray Harryhausen used stop-motion and incredible models to breathe life into fantasy films throughout the fifties, sixties, and seventies. "You know these things aren't alive but they *look* like they are," said Chris.

Being able to see the fruits of your labor unveiling before your eyes is one of the appeals of stop-motion, especially with the use of digital photography. "I think creative people need reward, even if it's just for ourselves," said Oscar-winner Michel Gondry, who is famous for using stop-motion, particularly in his LEGO music video for The White Stripes. "Doing animation and watching the completed shot, it's a great reward—it gives you the energy to do the next one."

WHAT IS A BRICK-FILM?

The term "brick-film" was first coined by Jason Rowoldt who founded the website Brickfilms.com in 2000. While some animators' definitions vary, Philip Heinrich, who runs the popular site bricksinmotion.com, says, "I would say it's a film featuring LEGO as the principal medium. Most of these films are stop-motion animation, of course, though I've seen good uses of live action and other techniques as well. There's an old debate about whether or not computer-animated films with LEGO characters should qualify. I feel like the distinctions aren't so important to define, though I certainly prefer to focus on stop-motion LEGO movies." For the purpose of this book, "brick-film" refers to films that incorporate LEGO and stop-motion animation in some way.

Some of the first unofficial brick-films were created by kids lucky enough to have cameras, and amateur animators who discovered and embraced LEGO's awesome animation properties (see Why Animate with LEGO? on page 26). One of those kids was Lars Hassing who filmed a six-minute film incorporating live action and stop-motion when he was twelve years old. The film was made as a present for his grandparents' golden wedding anniversary in 1973, and was eventually seen by LEGO's CEO Godtfred Kirk Christiansen. Turn to page 16 for an in-depth look at the film.

Some of the earliest on-screen stop-motion with LEGO can be seen in the animation classic *The Wizard of Speed and Time.* This low-budget feature film, produced in 1989, was written, directed, and animated by the film's star, Mike Jittlov. The film is about a special effects "wizard" who is trying to make a feature film in Hollywood. The movie incorporates many impressive stop-motion techniques and features a few brief moments where classic LEGO Space sets come to life.

LEGO launch—shots of the space shuttle take-off and the town plan from Lars Hassing's 1973 brick-film, *Journey to the Moon*.
© Lars Hassing

For many animators, however, there is one short film that has stood the test of time and is considered the original brick-film, and that is *The* *Magic Portal* by Australian animator Lindsay Fleay. Filmed over a four-and-a-half-year period while Lindsay majored in film and television at

LEGO on the loose—from the set of Lindsay Fleay's masterpiece *The Magic Portal*.
© Lindsay Fleay

college, this sixteen-minute stop-motion film incorporates LEGO, card, Plasticine, and live-action footage and was funded in part by the Australian Film Commission. The film is as complete a bible for LEGO stop-motion as exists, and incorporates many of the techniques suggested in this book. *The Magic Portal* is all the more impressive given the fact it was shot in the late 1980s, without many of the cheats and aids animators can rely on today. Animator Tony Mines sums it up when he says, "The reason I really love this film is—for me—it's a microcosm of the whole brick-film evolution. When it starts out, you think it's going to be just another kid-level brick-film, with stud-walking and uninventive basic set building, but by the end of the thing it's gone pretty

Two of the characters from *The Magic Portal* on board their space craft.
© Lindsay Fleay

13

much everywhere—moving cameras, replacement mouths, blob monsters depicted with sequential brick swapping, color-swapping as special effect, flat-surface walking animation mixed with live action. . . . It basically stands as a postmodern meta-narrative on a whole school of filmmaking. It simultaneously invents and deconstructs. It's kind of the true *2001: A Space Odyssey* of LEGO animation, the alpha and omega." Turn to page 21 for an interview with the director, Lindsay Fleay.

The Magic Portal may have remained one of the most revered brick-films over the years, but it's not well known beyond LEGO stop-motion circles. In 1999 a film called *Rick and Steve: The Happiest Gay Couple in All the World* was doing the film festival rounds—a LEGO stop-motion comedy about exactly what it said on the tin. The couple in question and their community were portrayed by LEGO minifigures, and while the short was well received by audiences, a subsequent lawsuit

A shot from competition-winning film *Jane's Brain* by Chris Salt
© Chris Salt

filed by LEGO meant it wasn't until 2007 that creator Q. Allan Brocka released a TV series of the same name. This time, the stop-motion puppets were not LEGO minifigures, although they retained similar joints and hinges as their Danish counterparts. The show has aired in the United States, Canada, the United Kingdom, and France and ran for two seasons.

Other animators whose unofficial LEGO offerings have received wider acclaim include Nate "Blunty" Burr and Chris Salt. Nate's LEGO music video for Jamie Kennedy and Stu Stone's "Circle Circle Dot Dot" has been viewed over 17.5 million times on YouTube. Stone also created the TV show *Meatspace,* which aired for six episodes as part of ABC's video gaming program *Good Game.* Chris Salt's various animations for BBC Radio 6 Music's *Adam and Joe Show* including *Jane's Brain,* which is covered in detail on page 188.

The first and only stop-motion LEGO film that Lars Hassing ever made was called *Journey to the Moon*, a golden wedding anniversary present for his grandparents that he created when he was just twelve years old. Filmed in 1973, it stands as a testament to what can be achieved with limited equipment, editing, and without computer-generated visual effects, as well as the ingenuity and creativity of children who play with LEGO.

What was it like to have the opportunity to create stop-motion films using your own toys as a child?

It was very exciting to have the opportunity to make a film. Only a few people had film cameras; my grandfather was one of them, and we borrowed it for two months in 1973 together with a 500W lamp. The camera was a Eumig Vienette

Super 8. The film came in a 3:20 minutes cartridge, which was rather expensive, at least for kids.

What was it like building and playing with LEGO prior to the introduction of specific themes, such as Space in the late 1970s?

Well, we just invented our own themes. We often built a railroad,

then sitting in each end of the room, we wrote small notes that were sent by train requesting bricks or ready-built cars from each other.

How did you discover the art of stop-motion?

It was a different age, forty years ago. There were no computers or smartphones to steal our time; the

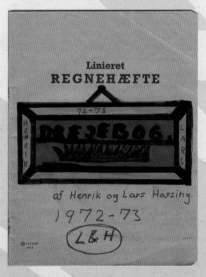
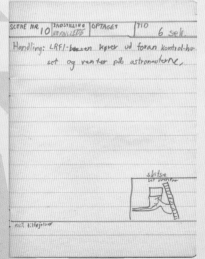
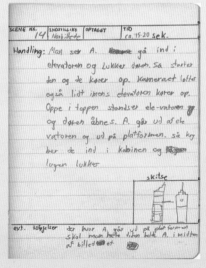

The "playbook" that Lars Hassing used to plan *Journey to the Moon*—the pages show scene numbers, storyboard sketches, and descriptions of the action.
© Lars Hassing

TV only had one channel in Denmark, so we had to entertain ourselves. That winter I had immersed myself in a thorough five-hundred-plus-page book about amateur filming, *Jeg smalfilmer*. Stop-motion looked exciting, and as LEGO was my big hobby, this was an easy way to provide the props. I was generally technically interested and another passion was the Apollo program that was happening at that time. I read every book I could get hold of, and knew the complete process of moon travel, every step of the journey. I built LEGO rockets with a Lunar Module inside and played the sequence, so it was an obvious theme for a film.

How much planning went into making *Journey to the Moon*?

The building of the LEGO houses and vehicles for the film took place over many weekends during the beginning of 1973; my cousin came over and we built in the basement of my parents' house. Later my little sister joined, helping create the landscapes in papier-mâché and painting them. The film was shot between March–April 1973 on the weekends. My parents granted us two 3:20 film cartridges, and as stop-motion takes a *very* long time, that was fine. We didn't have access to cutting—only a simple splicing of the two films—so I made a

detailed storyboard and the film was shot sequentially.

What was your favorite stop-motion technique that you employed in the film?

I've always thought it looked cool when the small LEGO people went down into the heli-jet to be transported to the aircraft carrier. The effect was made by removing the bottom brick of the figure, one for each frame. The figures used in the film were made using 1 × 1 bricks, as minifigures had not been invented yet.

Lars (center) shooting the town scene at the beginning of the film.
© Lars Hassing

Setting fire on film for the explosive launch effect.
© Lars Hassing

There's one scene where you set fire to the LEGO to recreate the space shuttle's launch—I can't imagine a lot of twelve-year-olds being allowed to do that today!

My father was not too happy about it, but we obviously managed to convince him that it was necessary for the film. I remember I picked some old and very worn bricks to be near the firecrackers. The ignition went well, we filmed for a few seconds, but then realized we hadn't thought about stopping the firecracker—so we just had to let it finish burning.

How did you feel when you saw the completed production?

Excited to show it to our grandparents, but we were somewhat disappointed by the lacking quality of the close-ups. We only had access to my grandfather's camera. We did observe the minimum distance from camera to scene, but nevertheless the result often was a bit blurred—too bad since we invested a lot of time.

Was the film shown at your grandparents' golden wedding anniversary party? What was their reaction to it?

Yes, it was shown at the party and they and their fifty guests were very surprised and impressed, never having seen anything like it, and especially as it was made by kids. Before and after the party my cousin and I spent many holiday weeks at their home, moving furniture to the walls of their living room, clearing the floor, and building LEGO all over.

Is it true that LEGO's CEO at the time, Godtfred Kirk Christiansen, also saw the film?

My grandfather was very proud of the film and definitely thought that LEGO should see it, so he wrote a letter and we got invited—my grandparents, my sister, my cousin, and I. We remember Godtfred as a big, smiling, friendly man in a white shirt with suspenders. We went to his office and then showed the film in a projector room. He was very interested and pleased with the film, and asked for a copy. Then we had a guided tour of the factory and received one of the largest LEGO sets of that year. Finally we received free tickets for LEGOLAND, where we spent the rest of the day.

***Journey to the Moon* was shot using a Eumig Vienette Super 8 camera. To watch the film go to www.youtube.com/user/lars chassing/videos.**

Here, part of the same set can be seen in the finished film.
© Lars Hassing

Filming the moon landing with LEGO in 1973.
© Lars Hassing

Official LEGO brick-films

LEGO has never made a full-length feature film using stop-motion, but they have commissioned a number of stop-motion shorts to help promote products. Spite Your Face Productions has been behind a few of the most high-profile of these films including *Spider-Man—The Peril of Doc Ock*, which is the very first LEGO animation to use fleshy minifigures, and *Monty Python and the Holy Grail in LEGO*. The Monty Python frame-for-frame recreation of the famous Camelot scene was made for Python Pictures and LEGO and was included on the *Monty Python and the Holy Grail* special edition DVD. The video has received over 2.5 million views online.

The Spider-Man film, made for LEGO, Sony, and Marvel, came out to promote the release of *Spider-Man 2* in 2004, and became a viral hit. Tony Mines, who created the film, was surprised that viewers didn't seem to notice the LEGO minifigures' new natural skin tones—Spider-Man sets were among the first to incorporate these along with Harry Potter and the official NBA sets. "I ascribe this to unintentional blindness," he explains. "It highlights a very important and fundamental lesson about animation. Animation is less about moving things from here to there to simulate motion, as it is about understanding how we see things and deliberately tricking us. In this case, the rest of the Spider-Man film goes so far to create a reality for the minifigures, placing you at their level in close-up and presenting them as human, that the very obvious incongruity of their color goes unnoticed."

How long does it take to make a brick-film?

This question is akin to asking, "How long is a piece of string?" Depending on your experience, your film idea, your equipment, your computer skills, and a number of other factors, your LEGO animation can be as long and take as long as you like. Some of the animations in this book were made in a couple of weeks, from conception to completion, while others took months or even years to complete. Although the length of your film can have a bearing on the length of your production—more shots will take more time to film—a complex thirty-second animation with special effects and visual effects could be a much larger project than you might imagine. Jonathan Vaughan is one animator who has dedicated many hours of his life to making stop-motion films.

"I'll spend weeks or months writing a script and revising it, then find voice actors, record the voices, and determine what parts or equipment I'll need to purchase to complete the film," Jonathan says. "I also usually storyboard the film before I begin filming. In the case of *Melting Point*, storyboarding alone took a few months because the film has over five hundred shots and extensive planning was required. In the past, I would often finish shooting a film only a few days before it was completely done. Now, however, months of postproduction work are required after shooting has completed."

As it's likely you will have other commitments—school, college, or a job—it's common for projects to span long time periods before completion.

Having a flexible shooting schedule is a good idea, so you can calculate how long the animation will take you and then factor in time for postproduction. That way you will be spurred on to meet your deadline. If you don't have much time to commit to the hobby, it's wise to stick to smaller projects that you can realistically complete, so you get the satisfaction of finishing.

What makes a great brick-film?

The brick-filming community is a largely positive, supportive group who are inspired by each other, and curious about techniques and tricks. Being a brick-filming success for some happens overnight. They post a short film with a great script, unique idea, or impressive special effect, and it goes viral. But remember, success comes in many guises. A video that has been viewed millions of times online doesn't necessarily translate to the best photography, the most complex animation, or the greatest story. The most important thing to remember about stop-motion is to enjoy the process and make something that you think is great. Adam Radwell, whose *Grease* animation is explored on page 141, says that passion is the key to success. "If you are passionate about making the animation then you are going to put time, effort, and love into it. No matter what skill level you are at, if you want it to turn out amazing, and are willing to go that extra mile and take the stress, frustration, and annoyance on the chin, then you will end up with an impressive end product. Not everyone is going to like what you make and you will always receive criticism. But if you are proud of it then, to me, that is a job well done!"

In 1985 Lindsay Fleay was studying film and television at Curtin University in Perth, Australia. This was the year that he also embarked on a four-year project to make *The Magic Portal,* considered by many to be the original brick-film and an inspiration for many of the animators in this book.

What was the initial inspiration for the film?

I wanted to make something entirely myself. It was also a continuation of my early Super8 stop-motion, some of which used LEGO, cardboard, and Plasticine. There was a simplistic LEGO forerunner to *The Magic Portal* called *LEGOMATIX* (1984) shot entirely on Super8, and it essentially became the dry run for *Portal.* Some of the main influences were the eighties arcade and C64 games, mostly how they moved and used things like parallax. There was also that radical new space created by games—it was like watching the birth of cinema, except I was *there* to watch it happen—and the big explosion in movies at the time. There were giant leaps in special effects and how movies were being made, with everything from *Alien* to *Tron* to the barrage of post-*Star Wars* effects and fantasy films.

As the film progressed, there was also a growing awareness of old movies, and the way that they were put together. Alfred Hitchcock would have been my prime obsession back then, especially since they re-released a whole pile of his classic works. Much of my cinematic language got honed here. There was also a strong TV and comic influence. Early *2000AD*—when it was still printed on newsprint—*Doctor Who* during the Tom Baker period, *The Goodies,* and *Monkey* would be the most obvious examples.

Why did you decide to make the film using LEGO? Had you seen the medium used elsewhere in this way?

As far as I knew back then, I was the only one. I felt LEGO too limiting at the time, and considered Meccano, but that proved even more tricky and convoluted, and I lacked experience and contacts to make it work. There were a few odd sods around, spending years obsessing about special effect shots or spending about a *decade* on some pet project. I did *not* want to end up like that so it was partly a pragmatic decision. It never occurred to me I was breaking any ground. I was simply using the materials at hand. I was making a stop-motion film; it just happened to have LEGO in it.

THE MAGIC PORTAL © 1989 LINDSAY FLEAY

Stepping through the portal into a weird and wonderful world.
© Lindsay Fleay

The 16mm Bolex and lighting setup for the film.
© Lindsay Fleay

What was the production process like?

There was a twelve-month period of hunting down funding, storyboarding, and testing. Animation was nearly entirely solo, shot in three to six week blocks, per 100-foot roll of film, around breaks, holidays, and weekends. For the most part, the bulk of it was shot over a nine-month period, but the editing and postproduction seemed to drag on forever. It was shot in our concrete basement—you see it in the final film—where I could control lighting somewhat, using homemade rigging and borrowed equipment from the university. A lot of the equipment was *ancient*. Most of the sets were shot on a tiny tabletop. The sets were modular, and were taken apart and rebuilt around the characters . . . for every frame.

The film incorporates a variety of stop-motion techniques, mixes materials, and includes live action to great effect. Did you have any concerns about their success while you were making it?

Not really. I had confidence in all of it, because I'd gone through a rigorous testing process and it was all approved, storyboarded and plotted out to some insane degree on reams of graph paper. The only concern I had really was not messing up and wasting precious film. Each roll would take about two to three weeks to shoot for the major LEGO scenes. I went through eleven of them. I had no way of previewing anything until it was all done. I relied on a light meter, some calculations, and careful measuring to get my exposure levels and focus together. Some characters are so big on screen that they almost touched the lens! I had to flood the set with light to get my focal length deep, working at f16, which mean the set kept warping under the heat of the lights in spite of all the fans, and I kept leaving fingerprints on the LEGO. It was all made possible with this amazing 10mm lens I had access to. It made the tiny sets detailed but not distorted, and the minfigs looked about a meter tall when it was screened.

Relying on your own calculations must have been nerve-racking, but an exciting experience when you saw the developed film. Were there any big surprises?

The film had to be posted to the lab on the other side of the country, which took about a fortnight, including processing. Then came the nerve-racking experience of opening up that film can, chopping the work print into pieces, and then watching the final thing jump off the screen. There were my storyboards, in livid color. It was magic. Nothing quite matches that sensation.

I had one roll malfunction, though. Roll three took three weeks

to shoot. It was mostly interior scenes and some of the big LEGO chase. I worked around the clock, trying to get it all done and posted off. Then when it returned a fortnight later . . . disaster. The claw mechanism had failed in the camera. I had four minutes of streaky color on my film. I vaguely recall staggering home, chucking a tantrum, kicking the house, and then slumping in a corner and crying my eyes out for forty-five minutes. Then I picked myself up, and reshot roll three all over again, from scratch, in two weeks.

A bit different from the instant results filmmakers get today . . .

When *The Magic Portal* was initially hosted by someone on YouTube, the idea of not previewing anything just simply didn't register. Describing the process of processing and cutting had some people think I was trolling them. The [members of the] forums barely knew what film was, apart from some old guys my

age. They had no idea of half the references in the film. I'm glad they restarted *Doctor Who* in 2005, because for a few years there, there were a lot of kids watching the film, scratching their heads about the Liquid Paper Daleks. Not that they'd ever experienced white-out fluid either.

How did you feel when the film was finally complete in 1989?

Relief. I couldn't actually believe it. At the time, as a young fella, four and a half years felt like a lifetime. I couldn't believe it was all over. It was a case of "Now what?" and finding a way to occupy myself. *The Magic Portal* did completely cure me of LEGO though. I was utterly obsessed with the stuff before. I'd achieved everything I'd set out to do, and surprised myself when it exceeded everything I'd expected with the final product. I'd brought it to life, created a world not unlike your childhood imagination, a place

Lindsay built the set so walls could be easily moved for camera access—note the fan for keeping the set cool under the lights, and the pile of different colored portals, which were switched in and out to create a flashing effect.
© Lindsay Fleay

that operates on its own internal rules and logic. What else was there to do? It was more successful than my wildest dreams.

Did you have the chance to screen the film at all and see the public's reaction?

I sourced a little rinky-dink distributor in Perth, which approached the LEGO Group. This is where I discovered I'd built this beautiful bridge in the middle of a desert. Anything to do with LEGO has the problem where it's essentially classified as advertising by just about every broadcaster on the planet, so there are issues with kids' TV and how much advertising you could show. While we negotiated with LEGO, we were held up for months as festivals slipped past. I think a

year or two later it was shown at one or two festivals in Australia, but its big release was being screened six times on SBSTV, the government-funded multicultural TV network in Australia. The proceeds from that funded my post-grad animation studies in Melbourne in 1990.

During those studies, I received my first fan mail from a twelve-year-old kid, who caught half the film on television. He tracked me down, invited me to his primary school to show it, and I had the extraordinary experience of inciting a seventy-strong six-year-old riot showing the film to all the juniors. It was amazing: they were practically climbing all over the TV, barraging me with questions and asking me in all seriousness whether I was a magician or not. That's when I realized this thing was bigger than just my

basement and that it wasn't mine anymore; they'd made it theirs. The morale boost got me through my studies, and living in poverty in Melbourne, and gave me my career kick start, although I didn't know it at the time.

How has your career been shaped by the experience of making this film?

It's informed everything. It's what I learned on. All the 3D animation throughout my career was treated as a virtual stop-motion set. I teach it that way too, when I can. What I really gained from The *Magic Portal* was a filmic language. Get that right, and everything else is cosmetic detail by comparison.

What advice would you have for those wanting to push the limits of what LEGO animation can do?

Invent everything as you go, solve all your problems as you go. It's not "old school", its "sensible school," as Ridley Scott says. There's a huge crowd of people out there who need to find a one-button app to solve their problems, or worse, they effectively delegate all their thinking to Google and Wikipedia. Without a proper context, it's a recipe for rapid self-extinction.

If you want to be a successful film-maker, then you need to somehow find a way to regulate the constant contact and communication with your live audience on the Internet, with the requirement of shutting yourself away and being a

THE MAGIC PORTAL © 1989 LINDSAY FLEAY

The Liquid Paper Daleks from *The Magic Portal*.
© Lindsay Fleay

thoroughly unsociable troglodyte, just to get something done. Discovering stuff and working in isolation were critical to making *The Magic Portal* unique. Not to mention what I call the Anvil of Boredom. Most of my motivation was to overcome sheer boredom. The slow pace also gave you a *lot* of contemplation time, so every decision I made, looking back on it, was fully considered, weighed, assessed and tempered. Every shot works because I agonized long and hard over it.

The problem with digital production is that you can perfectly realize the first stupid thing that springs to mind and that's why you get a lot of awesome-looking stupidity these days. It becomes a short circuit. Worse, it's disposable instant gratification. Avoid lots of hits—go for influential instead. It takes time to make good stuff. And good stuff lasts, I'm happy to report. Just hang in there!

The Magic Portal was shot on a 16mm windup Bolex, without the use of a motor drive or remote trigger. It was edited by hand on Steenbeck flatbed editors and picsyncs. The film is available on YouTube and you can find out more about Lindsay Fleay at www.rakrent. com.

WHY ANIMATE WITH LEGO?

Apart from the rather obvious answer of, "Because LEGO bricks are amazing and animating with them is a super fun time, thank you very much!" there are a number of very practical reasons why you might choose to animate LEGO toys over other mediums. As explored earlier in the book, LEGO is not the only material you can use to create stop-motion videos, but for a beginner the level of ingenuity and creativity already instilled in LEGO products

Just some of the many moving parts LEGO has produced over the years.
© Paul Hollingsworth

means rather than starting from scratch, you literally have the building blocks for a slick animation at your fingertips. And it's not just amateurs who recognize the simplicity and potential of LEGO bricks—professional animators are also getting in on the act. "LEGO was the first thing I tried to animate purely because I happened to have some on hand," said Chris Salt. "It's great for a beginner because the stud system makes it hard to mess up too badly—as long as you remember which stud a minifig was standing on, you can pick him up, move his arms and legs around, and put him back down again and know that he'll be in pretty much the same place as in the previous frame."

But the reliable stud system is only one reason LEGO really is the best animation tool to start you on your stop-motion journey. Here are a few more.

Affordability

When compared to the cost of producing professional armatures like those used in stop-motion feature films and television programs, LEGO toys are a considerably more affordable option, especially for someone wanting to try out the medium for the first time or for younger filmmakers with less money in their piggy banks. While the bill for lots of LEGO, especially when buying specific parts from sites such as bricklink.com, can make your eyes water, a lot can be achieved with a relatively small collection, and film ideas can easily be scaled to suit an individual's budget.

ABS

No, we're not talking about glistening six-packs—those three letters stand for acrylonitrile butadiene styrene, which has been the type of plastic used to make LEGO bricks and parts since 1962. Under the advice of Swiss engineer, Hans Schiess, the company made the switch from using cellulose acetate to ABS because he recognized its colorfast, durable nature, its strength, and that it was easy to mold accurately in small amounts—ideal for the high-quality, tiny bricks the company wanted to produce.

This lasting high quality has become synonymous with LEGO products, and has in part helped to stave off the advances of cheaper competitors. Add to that ABS's light weight, resilience under pressure and heat, and you can rest assured your models won't melt or warp under the hot lights of your animation studio, won't bend or break hours into filming a crucial, detailed scene, but will allow you the flexibility to achieve the moment you want as precisely as you want it.

Reusability

Animator Zach Macias prefers using LEGO as an animation tool over clay and other puppets, claiming it's easier and cheaper. "With clay, resources for models and sets can only be used once, and then once it's used, you must go out and purchase more materials to make more things that will only be used a few times at the most before they need to be stored or scrapped," he says. "LEGO, on the other hand, is very flexible in that sets and characters can easily be constructed, deconstructed, reconstructed, and repurposed for your specific needs. The small-scale size can sometimes be a bit of a challenge to work with, but the ability to, say, tear down a wall and move a set over a few studs in order to achieve a certain camera angle, or borrowing parts from one set to complete another, make the already-tedious process of stop-motion a little less difficult."

Joints and hinges

While not intended as a product for stop-motion, the quality of ABS used, combined with the LEGO Group's rigorous quality control processes, mean that each LEGO brick, part, and minifigure can be relied on to perform the same functions precisely and identically to its counterparts for a lifetime, if not longer. A minifigure's arm, for example, can be posed and held at any point around the 360-degree axis of its shoulder. And with six points of articulation, and hands that can hold objects, the LEGO minifigure offers a range of accurate movement to convey meaning and tell a story, which is unparalleled by comparable toys. And tiny yellow arms are just the beginning—over its history LEGO parts have included a dizzying number of hinges, joints, wheels, and other articulated pieces which can be used to improve the movability of your LEGO movie.

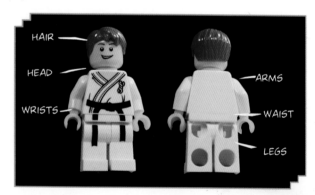

LEGO minifigures might be simple, but they sure can move—wrists, arms, heads, hair, waists, and legs can all be manipulated to bring life to your characters.
© Paul Hollingsworth

A LEGO world

Dozens of themes and sub-themes and a growing range of licensed lines have resulted in a widely available, hugely varied universe of locales, parts, and characters in the LEGO universe. From the superheroes of the Marvel and DC Comics pantheons to Paradisa ponies and Classic Space ships and astronauts, you're sure to find the characters you need in this eclectic, ready-made casting call. And if you can't, then mix and match minifigure parts to your heart's content or order custom minifigures, weapons, and accessories online from sites like firestartoys.com, minifigs.me, or brickforge.com. Existing LEGO sets provide you with a great starting point if building is not your forte or you just want to get on with animating, but for a LEGO animation that's all your own, you can build every location exactly how you imagine it.

A design classic

LEGO bricks and minifigures are design icons recognized around the world. By incorporating them into your films you invite your audience into a realm they are familiar with, allowing you to subvert, fulfill, or confuse their expectations. Disbelief is easily suspended for the minifigure people inhabiting your film's world, enabling the audience to immediately connect to the story you are telling rather than focusing on the absurdity of these little plastic people. Or as Chris Salt put it: "I think there's just something inherently silly about seeing what these iconic, stocky little plastic men get up to. A lot of the hard work in making them charming and funny has already been done by LEGO."

The sophisticated design of LEGO bricks and parts makes it hard for your sets and characters *not* to look good. The measured nature of the stud and tube system makes animating easier to control and master and encourages a methodical and mechanical approach to building and deconstruction—ideal for someone getting to grips with stop-motion.

Limitations

As with every medium there are inevitably a few downsides. For some animators, the rigidity of LEGO might be too much of a restraint. But if you want to work with LEGO it's best to see the straight lines and sharp corners of plastic bricks as a creative challenge. LEGO fans have been building astonishing things from the medium for years and there's no reason that shouldn't be the same with your films. You, like Chris Salt, might find yourself having a complex relationship with those delightful little bits of plastic. "Designing characters and building new sets for each project is cheap and easy and it's a recognizable product that people have a real fondness for," he says. "On the other hand, the fixed shapes of the bricks and minifigs impose certain boundaries on what you can do. Just try picking up a phone without bending your elbow and you'll see what I mean."

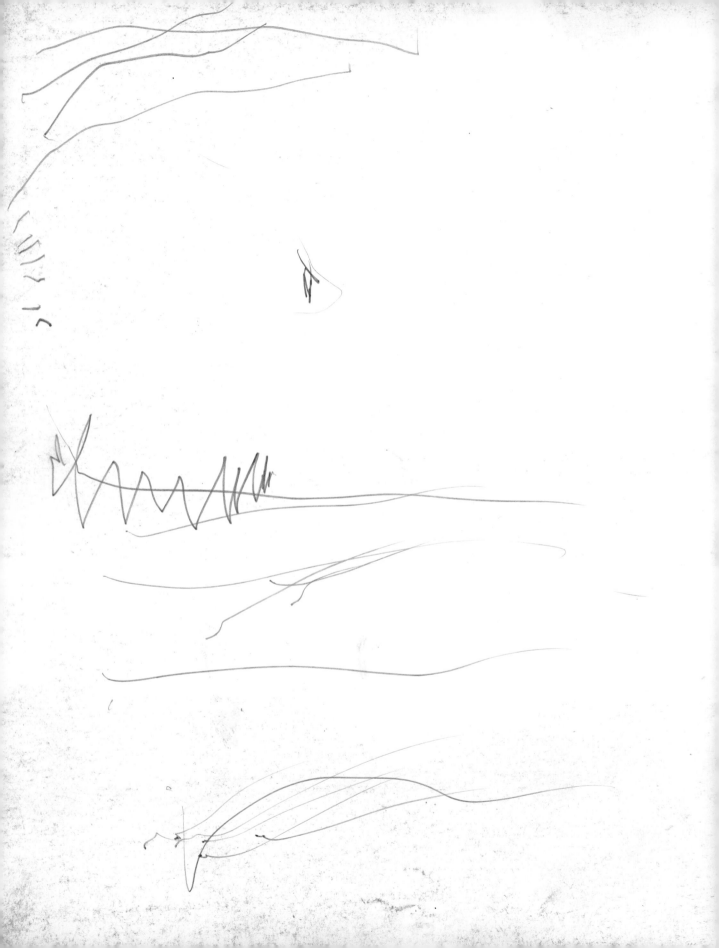

GETTING STARTED

2

As with any creative endeavor, there are a range of approaches to stop-motion animation that require the use of varying levels of equipment and materials. In the same way that LEGO bricks are not the only model subject for animators, the space and equipment used to film and edit can be varied. From webcams to expensive DSLR cameras and desk lamps to professionally lit studios, a lot of what you use depends largely on your budget, space, and personal preference.

This chapter aims to show you how best to set up your space for the optimum stop-motion experience. It will guide you through the essential equipment required to make a film and how to use it. If you want more than a basic setup, it also details everything you might need to help achieve movie-quality results.

While some might want to know how to take their hobby to the next level, there will be many readers starting out who are apprehensive about spending lots of money on fancy equipment. It's important to remember that affordable cameras and software are capable of producing fantastic results if you put the time and energy into your animations. There's no point parting with thousands of dollars on a high-end product to make a film you could produce just as well with what you already have. Many award-winning animated films, shorts, and music videos were made on the same affordable cameras and software that you have at home. It's not always the equipment you have, but what you do with it that matters.

UNDERSTANDING YOUR STOP-MOTION SETUP

How you decide to arrange your studio is personal preference, but there are four technical elements you would expect to find in a stop-motion setup: a camera to take the images, a computer to capture and compile the images, software capable of collecting the images into a playable sequence to enable you to animate effectively, and a connection between the camera and the computer.

Camera

In the twenty-first century, we are never far from a lens—whether it's on our phone, computer, or a more traditional camera. Just about any camera is capable of taking a sequence of images that could then be turned into an animation, but what animators rely heavily on is the ability for their camera to export a live video feed to their computer. This means they can play back the sequence of images as they're taking them, or view the change between images in real time. This feature is standard on most video camcorders and webcams, but if you're choosing to use a digital stills camera, you should check to be sure it's included. For more on choosing a camera turn to page 35.

Computer

As mentioned previously, one of the main roles of a computer in animating this way is to capture the individual frames as they are taken and compile them into a sequence and video file. This file can then be uploaded immediately or opened in an editing program along with other files to make a finished film. The general age, speed, and individual components of your existing computer (or any you are buying specifically for animation) will, as with any IT task, affect the ease with which you can work on your production. But unless you're planning on making a three-hour LEGO epic, any fairly decent, relatively new computer should be enough to get you started.

Software

The two types of software you want to consider for your setup are some kind of stop-motion animation software and editing software. As mentioned previously, the former will allow you to review and edit your progress as you go, taking frames directly from your camera. This is ideal as it allows you to spot changes you want to make—and mistakes you don't—right away, rather than after you've already moved or dismantled your set. It will also enable you to compile your frames into relevant image sequences, to speed up your editing process, and to export your sequences as video files. If you don't have live video feed capabilities on your camera, then stop-motion animation software could still be worth using for reading and compiling images and reordering them into a more usable sequence.

If you're looking to compile multiple sequences, add sound and/or special effects, then you're going to need some editing software too. More on this on page 42.

Connection

Ideally, your camera will have a live video feed and will be connected to your computer, which will be running stop-motion animation software. From there you will be able to photograph each frame remotely, and play them back as an animation. This means you won't have to touch your camera between setups, which is vital for avoiding the tiny movements that will show up if you do. The type of connections will vary from model to model, but your typical USB connection that you might already use for downloading photographs should do the job.

Stop-motion animation software like Dragonframe has a cinematography workspace for setting up your shot and adjusting settings, and an animation workspace to see how your film is progressing.
© Paul Hollingsworth

CHOOSING A CAMERA

With the myriad of camera options available, it can be hard to know what you need, and how much to spend, to achieve the results you're looking for. To start animating right away, your main concern should be a camera that can export a live video feed to your computer. This might be a camcorder, a digital camera, or a webcam.

A lot of cheaper devices, and even some more costly ones, are going to eventually have issues that you might find problematic, especially if you're hoping to achieve a professional finish. One such problem is that of "flicker"—an uneven fluctuation in the quality or amount of light that the camera captures from one frame to the next.

Practice makes perfect and often simple problems can be fixed by understanding your equipment better. Make sure you read your camera manual, and search online for other users who may have experienced similar problems for a solution before you throw in the towel. In some cases, the quality of the product will be its downfall and that's something you can't change. To avoid the problem, you may want to think about upgrading to a higher spec to suit the quality of film you want to make.

To make those purchasing decisions a little less painful, we've come up with a list of features and functions that you should look for in any camera you're hoping to use for stop-motion. This is by no means a definitive list of all the useful and clever functions that are available, but can be used as a shopping guide for your new camera, a troubleshooting guide for your existing camera, and as a rule of thumb for the optimum settings you will want to use.

Manual settings

If stop-motion animation is the art of moving objects one picture at a time, stop-motion photography is the art of keeping everything else still! The last thing you want in the middle of a successful animation session is to have the set move, or the camera move, or anything else that isn't supposed to move, move. Even a small catastrophe can set you back hours. This also goes for unexpected changes in your camera's settings, so the more manual control options are available and active in your camera, the better suited it will be to stop-motion. Essentially, you want a camera that can take *exactly* the *same* picture hundreds of

© Paul Hollingsworth

times, with not even the slightest tiny difference between them, except for the moves you make to your model. So if nothing else, remember the mantra; "Manual settings, manual settings, manual settings!"

Live preview/video out

For most cameras, this live feed will be the source of the images you will use in your final film, but certain high-end SLR cameras will give you the option of a second higher quality image source. With this function your stop-motion animation software will be able to capture a live feed as a video assist—a video screen on your computer

that shows you the video action as it happens, which will aid you in your animation—and at the same time take high-res digital photos that you could then use in your final edit. This is the way professional TV and film productions work.

Exposure simulation video

After stressing the importance of manual settings, it's essential to make sure that if you're going to use a live feed as a video assist, you want the high-res images you're also capturing to match up identically to what you're using as a guide—namely the same film speed/ISO, shutter speed, and aperture settings. This requires your camera to offer exposure simulation, sometimes referred to as "exposure priority display," which ensures your manual settings of choice apply to both the video feed and the photography settings.

Manual film speed/ISO, shutter speed, and aperture settings

Film speed or ISO is a measure of a photographic film's sensitivity to light. In digital cameras this is recreated by the "sensor speed." Shutter speed refers to the length of time your camera's shutter remains open, letting the light in (e.g., a longer shutter speed or exposure used at night might help to brighten up the sky or create trails of light from passing cars). In animation, having the ability to control the shutter speed gives you more creative flexibility and longer exposures are essential for seeing what you're doing (see depth of field on page 66). Aperture—the size of the hole where the light gets in—works with the shutter speed to determine the exposure. If either of the two alters from frame to frame, you will notice flicker in your animations, which will prevent the sequence of frames from feeling like one continuous shot.

Manual aperture lens

For those wanting to banish flicker forever and create truly professional-looking films, it's probably a good idea to invest in a manual aperture lens for your camera, although this isn't essential for creating simple stop-motion films. Digital lenses on DSLRs will close to slightly different positions for each shot, even with manual settings. This is only really noticeable in stop-motion or time-lapse photography, and might only become apparent in low-lit shots. By adding a manual lens to your camera you can override the digital functions and make sure your aperture stays at a fixed position.

Do I need a DSLR?

Taking up stop-motion as a hobby, and wanting to get the best results, could mean you end up spending hundreds, possibly thousands of dollars to buy cameras, lights, software, and LEGO. As you'll see throughout the book there are lots of free and affordable options that will still produce great results, so knowing where to spend your money is important. When Daniel Utecht got into stop-motion for the first time, he thought a DSLR was an essential part of that package and coughed up the cash, but now he says that he could have saved himself the money. "I didn't do much research," he admits. "I didn't spend much time thinking, should I really spend $700 or $800 on a camera just for a hobby. Now that I know more and I've looked online, there are some good webcams like the Logitech C910, which is popular because it allows for manual settings. It's important to be able to manually set the settings and the camera focus, and take the photos without touching the camera. You can find a good webcam for animating for around one hundred dollars. The nice thing about webcams too is that they're smaller. The DSLR camera I use is very large, which can be tricky sometimes because LEGOs aren't too big themselves. The smaller the camera, the better, I would say."

Having a live preview while you animate can avoid mistakes and speed up the process.
© Paul Hollingsworth

Camera recommendation

Technological advancements mean it's pretty likely that all of the features described in this section will become standard in digital cameras before long. The films featured in this book utilize an array of different cameras, some possibly similar to what you own already, from Logitech webcams to Canon and Nikon DSLRs. If you want the best possible results and have the money to spend on a high-end camera, some combination of a Canon EOS digital single lens reflex camera (such as the 5DII, 5DIII, 7D, or 550D) with a manual aperture lens (such as a Nikon) would be a good investment. The top end of the EOS range is favored by professional animators all over the world.

Kevin Sarp's video, *Death Star Canteen*—a LEGO retelling of a popular joke by British comedian Eddie Izzard—was shot using a basic digital camera, no tripod, and a rudimental lighting setup. It's been viewed over twenty-one million times on You-Tube, making it one of the most watched LEGO animations of all time.

Darth Vader in the Death Star Canteen in Kevin's popular brick-film.
© Kevin Sarp

What advice would you give to other animators wanting to use part of a stand-up routine as their subject matter?

You should be creative in your interpretation and representation of jokes. Don't be afraid to add little things, like stormtroopers in the background, and try to come up with visual representations of strange concepts.

The film's small set during production.
© Kevin Sarp

How did using Eddie Izzard jokes as a basis for brick-films come about?

At first I was thinking about making music videos, something that LEGO has been used for a lot in the past. I was looking through my iPod for a good song to use and I saw Izzard's jokes. I decided to go with that, because comedy is a popular genre on YouTube, and his jokes provide clear visual images to work from.

Why do you think jokes lend themselves well to this medium?

Izzard's jokes are very visual, and often involve characters. I think there's also something inherently funny about serious characters like James Bond or Darth Vader portrayed as toys.

Describe the space that you use to animate.

My studio space is pretty simple. I use a desk in a well-lit room with another lamp directly on the desk and outside the view of the camera. I surround the desk lamp with upright

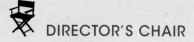

DIRECTOR'S CHAIR

Kevin Sarp's setup for *Death Star Canteen* was simple, but he kept everything in place (including hats) with electric tape, and built walls that were easy to remove so he could film from both sides of his set.
© Kevin Sarp

lined paper (held up by LEGO pillars, of course) to soften the light, which prevents glare on the shiny LEGO surfaces. The set is taped down and the camera is taped down in front of the set. This is the same setup I've used since starting, excluding small adjustments.

What useful thing should all brick-filmmakers have?

Electric tape. This simple tool is incredibly useful for making LEGO animations. Everything which doesn't move in your video must be secured during shooting. Electric tape will securely hold your set to your work surface, as well as secure any LEGO props which don't connect with their studs, such as things on wheels. What's great about electric tape specifically is that it's strong enough to hold LEGO down for filming, but won't leave glue on your LEGO bricks.

Do you use any tools, such as storyboards, to plan your film?

I don't write down or storyboard any of the video before filming. I usually form a basic idea of how each shot will look by listening to my selected audio clip several times, and then work out details as I go along. This works well for me, but it's a somewhat messy approach, so others may benefit from storyboarding. Coincidentally, this is somewhat similar to how Izzard does his shows; he doesn't write anything down either!

What tips have you picked up that you think others should know about?

- Tape hats to heads to make it easier to move the two pieces together to represent talking.
- Build the walls of your sets in sections, so that they can be removed for the camera to look through at different angles.
- Move your set to change angles, not your camera, so that your camera can remain secured in place.
- Make your characters move their arms, bodies, and heads while talking. Mouths can't move to show speech, so you need to show it by different methods.

- Once you've chosen what joke you want to use, edit the sound into an mp3 file and play the file on a loop as you're shooting so that you gain a close familiarity with each line's wording and timing. This will help your frames more closely match the audio with minimal editing.

How do you feel about the finished film and its popularity?

I was certainly quite surprised by its popularity. I'm glad I can add something valuable to many people's Internet experience, even if it is just LEGO. I think I'm most proud of the fact that Izzard himself has seen it and likes it. I almost made a remake for one of his DVDs, but it got cancelled because of legal trouble.

***Death Star Canteen* was made in 2007 and shot on a Canon Powershot A450. Kevin edited it using Windows Movie Maker. To watch the film and see his other Eddie Izzard LEGO videos, go to www.youtube.com/user/Thorn2200.**

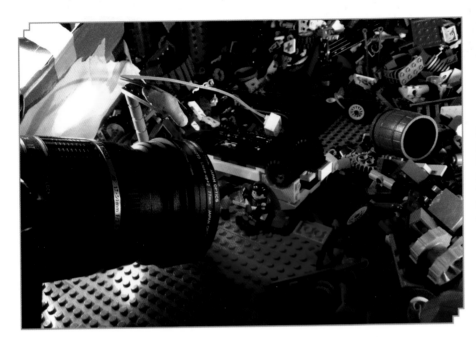

DSLR cameras and macro lenses are great for capturing LEGO sets in HD detail, but aren't necessary if you just want to have a bit of brick-filming fun.
© Jonathan Vaughan.

Working with what you've got

Having a professional set up would be a dream come true for most amateurs, but that doesn't mean that great films can't be achieved with the bare minimum, as Christian Colglazier explains: "I started out with very little in terms of a studio. My first brick-film was made by placing the sets on the carpet and using a point and shoot camera on a mini tripod. I soon upgraded to a desk set up with two desk lamps and a webcam. I stayed with this set up for several years and it worked really well. Once more money came my way, I was able to upgrade to a DSLR. The DSLR opened the door to do more artistic things in my films. The quality was significantly better. I also had the ability to play with more dramatic lighting."

STOP-MOTION ANIMATION SOFTWARE

There are a number of different software packages available to help you capture your images and animate efficiently. If you're going to spend money on a program, check in advance if it offers all the essential features outlined in this section—these are standard in programs such as Dragonframe and Stop Motion Pro, used by a number of the animators in this book. These professional-quality programs also include hundreds of other features not detailed here, which you can read about on their websites: www.dragonframe.com and www.stopmotionpro.com. If you just want to try things out first, there are a number of fairly proficient affordable and free programs you can download such as The Helium Frog Animator, iStopMotion, and AnimatorHD. While stop-motion animation software can include some editing features, it by no means replaces the need for an editing package (covered in chapter seven).

Frame capture

The most basic function of this software, as outlined earlier, is to take a frame from the live video feed, record it as an image and store it, adding it to a series of frames to create a sequence—your animation. Essentially, you press a button and a frame is taken, you press the button again and your next frame is taken, and so on.

Frame capture from multiple sources

This is the software's ability to capture the live video feed while simultaneously capturing digital photos of a better quality to use in your final film. These high-res images are too large for the instant playback you'll want when animating, so you view the much lower res ones from the video feed as your reference. Remember, not all cameras will allow you to utilize this option, even if the software is capable of handling it.

Device control

This "camera window" in the software will enable you to see all of your attached device's functions and make manual changes on your computer to your camera, so you can avoid touching your camera altogether throughout the animating process—perfect for setting ISO, exposure, and focus. The software should come with a list of the camera models it supports, so be sure to check this first.

Replay/playback

Reviewing your work as you go is the most efficient way to animate. Your software should give you the ability to instantly play back your frames and move between frames in sequence (your current frame and the previous two), or in reverse—allowing you to see how the animation is progressing and whether you've made any errors, so you can correct them right away.

Edit as you go

These features will enable you to edit as you go—deleting the last few frames or a single frame earlier in the sequence. Some software might offer advance

timeline options so you can reorder frames as you animate, duplicate them, or loop them. All of these functions will cut down the amount of time you have to spend in postproduction.

Onionskin

As you may imagine from the name, the onionskin function lets you see a semitransparent version of the previous frame or multiple frames over the live feed, so you can see how your next movement(s) will look in sequence while you adjust it. This function should have toggle and opacity options to suit your needs. Auto-toggle will flash between the live view and the capture frame.

Your software should allow you to edit as you go, deleting unwanted frames while you're animating.
© Paul Hollingsworth

TOP TIP—AVERAGING AWESOMENESS

"If your scene is static, and all the images captured for each frame are basically identical, you will have a nice clean frame," said Tony Mines. "But if something moves or falls over while the frame is being averaged, you may see a blurred image of the object progressively falling. This can be used to create all sorts of effects, like motion blur, by forcing slow, deliberate moves during the averaging process. Try taking a frame and then slowly edging a car a few millimeters forward while the software takes the shots."

Multiple frames can be seen using the onionskin feature in Dragonframe, helping you to accurately adjust your characters for the next shot.
© Paul Hollingsworth

Rotoscope layer

You might have heard the term "rotoscope" before—it traditionally referred to when animators trace over an image. This function will allow you to import and load up another video that can be layered over your animation to use as a guide. It might be a previous scene you've shot, a 2D reference drawing, or a movie or music video clip you're trying to match frame for frame. A video-rotoscope layer will play backward and forward frame by frame, progressing with your animation.

Frame averaging

If you're capturing your final images from the live feed, you might notice that there is a lot of "noise" in the image—jittery pixels that dance around in the darker areas of your frame, caused by image compression. This can often be even more noticeable than the kind you see in regular video footage, especially with a lower-quality video source like a webcam, camcorder, or phone. Frame averaging helps to solve this problem.

The feature means that each single click captures a set number of frames (determined by you) and averages them to create a single image. The more frames you set, the less "noise" in your final image. Keep in mind that using this feature means it will take a few more seconds to capture each frame, but will dramatically improve the final look of the images, as well as help to reduce flicker created by nonprofessional lights.

Organizing/filing

Even a small stop-motion film will require hundreds of frames and keeping all that organized on your own is quite a challenge. Luckily, most stop-motion animation software will automatically catalog your images for you. Dragonframe, for example, will create folders for your video feed, your high-res camera frames, and a backup, from the moment you open a new project and take your first shot.

Time-lapse function

This function lets you capture frames automatically at regular timed-intervals, creating time-lapsed footage—useful for including real time-lapsed skies or plants into your film, or other creative effects.

Timeline editing

While you're unlikely to find any stop-motion animation software that fulfills your editing needs, timeline editing means you can combine and edit multiple sequences ready to export. If you're new to the hobby, this is a great way to see your animation techniques realized without having to spend hours in postproduction.

Export compatibility

It's important that when you've finished animating a sequence you can export it at the quality you want in the format that you require—whether you're moving it to an editing package, or adding VFX (visual effects), your software should be versatile enough to meet your needs.

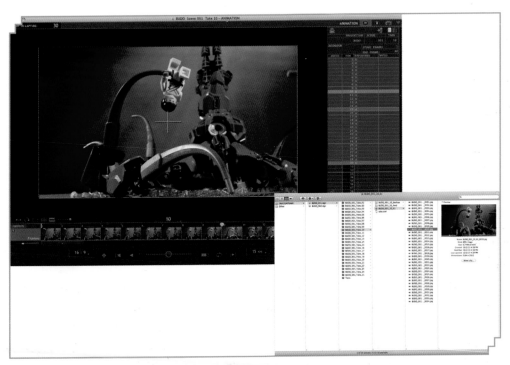

Automatic cataloging will help keep your production process organized and on schedule.
© Paul Hollingsworth

YOUR BASIC CAMERA SETUP

Now you know the basics of what you need in terms of a computer, camera, and connection, let's take a glance at how your setup should be looking. Use this checklist to make sure you're on the right track.

Cameras with video-only setup

1. Your video camera or webcam is set to all the available manual settings.

2. You have an appropriate cable connecting your camera's video export to your computer (this might be a USB or through the video-in port on your computer).

3. The camera is plugged in to the mains, with any automatic shutdown options disabled so your camera keeps working as long as you need it to.

4. Your stop-motion software is recognizing the live video feed via its device detection functions

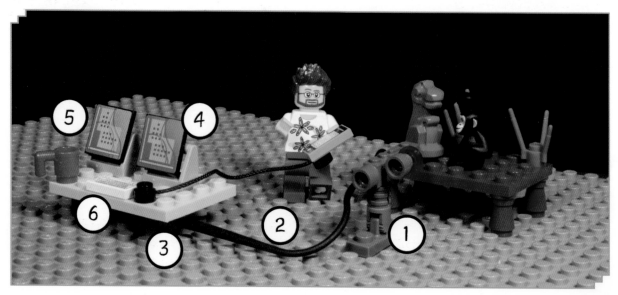

© Paul Hollingsworth

and you can see both your device control functions and your animation window on your computer, allowing you to control the camera while animating. You've also set up your software for frame averaging to cut out on any image noise and flicker.

5. Your computer is positioned away from your set so that screen glow won't affect the scene you're shooting.

6. You can use your keyboard shortcuts to avoid pressing any buttons near to the set.

© Paul Hollingsworth

Digital stills setup

In addition to the video-only setup from the previous image:

1. Your DSLR camera is set to all the available manual settings.

2. A manual aperture lens is attached to the camera via an adapter, disabling digital aperture functions.

3. You might have a custom keypad device to help you capture images on set, provided by your software manufacturer.

3
LIGHTING YOUR SET

Lighting is an element of **LEGO** stop-motion that can quite easily project your video from good to great. For some, lighting will be as simple as making sure that the set is lit enough to see the models and characters clearly, but often this can result in a poor quality, where the images captured on your camera do not do justice to the models you've built and can affect an audience's reaction to your film. This chapter explores the various techniques you can employ should you wish to create a more professional feel using lighting, though this does not necessarily require that you purchase studio-quality equipment. These tips are universal no matter the quality of equipment you are using. They also serve as general photography lighting tips, which you could apply to photographing stills of your MOCs–the **LEGO** fan acronym for a model you've designed and constructed yourself; it stands for "my own creation"–or for non-**LEGO** photography projects. It's also worth noting that following these guides should help to reduce the chance of some of the hazards associated with lighting your own set.

SAFETY FIRST

Shooting your own LEGO film should be a fun endeavor above all else. Causing harm to yourself or those around you in the pursuit of stop-motion animation might seem unlikely, but using electrical lighting can be hazardous, and it's not unusual to hear stories of filmmakers who have burned their hands on hot lights, or worse. Here are some top tips for making sure your LEGO, your house, and most importantly *you,* stay safe.

- Avoid touching lightbulbs and the metal housing that surrounds them. If you need to change a bulb or adjust something, make sure the equipment is completely cool, that is, it has been turned off for at least one hour, before touching.
- Try to avoid placing any objects or materials directly onto lightbulbs, lamps, or their metal housing.
- Where possible, always set up your lighting using reflectors and diffusion (see the following pages) to avoid direct lighting that can cause damage to your eyes.
- With a computer, camera, and a lighting setup, you might be using quite a large number of electrical devices at any one time. Make sure you don't overload a single plug socket, and if necessary use extension cables to spread out your device use across your room's electrical points. This is essential for a safe shoot, but will also reduce the chance of any electrical problems, which could save you time and effort.
- Try to use lights that produce little or no heat, like LEDs. These might be more costly at first, but they are safer to use, a better value as they last a lot longer, and are more eco-friendly than incandescent lightbulbs.
- If you're a younger filmmaker, it's always a good idea to get an adult to check out your setup before you get started. That can put your (and their) mind at ease so you can get on with making your movie in peace.

EXPOSURE

I f this word has you thinking about going out in the sun without sunscreen, you're not far off. As we explained earlier in the Camera section, exposure traditionally refers to the amount of light that the film inside a camera is exposed to when a photo is being taken. In digital photography it refers to the amount of light reaching the sensor. Using the manual settings described earlier, you are able to have a great amount of control over the exposure, but lighting also plays a key part in determining if an image is under- or overexposed.

An overexposed image will occur when too much light has reached the sensor and will result in the photograph being too bright—the lighter elements of the photograph losing definition, and the subject looking washed out. In contrast, an underexposed image will appear shadowy and dark. Well-placed lighting, diffusers, and a good understanding of your camera's manual settings can help you to eliminate the risk of these problems in your photos.

BOUNCING LIGHT

One key way to reduce overexposure is by bouncing the light onto your subject. Rather than pointing lights directly at whatever you're photographing, use reflectors that "bounce" the light toward your set. Reflectors can be made from a wide range of cheaply available items, many of which you probably have lying around. Try using a piece of white card or even paper, polystyrene panels, or mirrored card. Try out different materials and see what works for you. White and reflective surfaces are ideal, but be sure not to use anything conductive, such as a metal surface.

A standard two-light ambient setup using reflectors and diffusers.
© Paul Hollingsworth

A three-light ambient setup using a roof reflector.
© Paul Hollingsworth

Animating can mean long hours up close with your set. By bouncing the light, you also avoid having bright lights shining directly in your face. Minifigures aren't keen on this either, as direct lights are the fastest way to heat up a set and your LEGO. Using large professional lights directly in this way can actually lead to a visible heat haze, which will distort your images, and if left long enough, might even melt some of your set.

Using reflectors

Reflectors not only help to create the more subtle bounced light effect but they can also help to brighten up dark corners and areas where it's hard for light to reach. It's a good idea to place reflective surfaces, be that white paper or white LEGO, into seen and unseen areas of a set, especially if you only have a few lights available to work with. You'll be amazed at the difference a few carefully positioned white bricks can make.

Have a go at these quick and easy ways to introduce reflectors into your scenes:

- If a character moves behind a large piece of LEGO furniture, such as a sofa, tape a strip of white paper to the back of the sofa.
- If a character is coming through a door, tape a strip of white paper to the side of the door the camera doesn't see.
- If you're filming a scene where the floor is out of shot, use a white baseplate or cover the floor in white LEGO plates.
- If you're shooting a close-up of a character or group of characters, try positioning reflectors on either side of them just out of the shot.
- The shape of LEGO minifigures' heads and bodies attract a lot of unwelcome reflections, which might detract from the realism you are trying to create. If you position your reflectors well, you can avoid the reflection of your bedroom in your minifigure's head.

DIFFUSING LIGHT

Diffusing your light source is another great way of reducing overexposure and the distracting reflections that are inevitable when you shine a light onto plastic. Similar to bouncing the light, placing a diffuser in front of the bulb means the light will be distributed more softly onto the subject, appearing to come from a larger source, rather than from a small bulb.

To diffuse light, you don't need anything more than some thin plain paper or white silk organza fabric, but there are obviously more costly photographic solutions you could invest in. Lots of stop-motion animators use grease-proof paper because of its weight and the amount of light that it lets through. Paper is a flammable material, and lights can get very hot, so it's important to remember that diffusers should always be placed several inches away from the bulb, and any materials used to hold them in place (tape, LEGO bricks, etc.) should not be attached to the bulb or metal housing of the light.

Some filmmakers will ignore this last point, and tape or peg their diffusers directly to their lights. If this is your only option, be sure to take breaks in between filming where you switch the lights off to let the paper cool down.

Always position your diffuser paper/material at a safe distance from your lamps.
© Paul Hollingsworth

A LEGO scene lit without diffusers (top) and with diffusers (bottom). Note how the light is softer, and spread more evenly across the right-hand image.
© Paul Hollingsworth

Build a simple diffuser using a rectangle hardboard frame, quilting hoop, or other construct, and tape or staple the semi-transparent material to it. That way you can easily fix and move the frame around your lighting setup. Experiment with various materials and the position of the diffuser in front of the light source to see how it affects the light on your set.

Director's Chair
Keshen8

Keshen8 started out making brick-films with a cardboard box desk, a mini DV camera, and no animation software. Now he makes hilarious shorts, often incorporating popular icons like Iron Man and the X-Men with a DSLR, Dragonframe, and all the trimmings. He's also collaborated with Bad Robot and Hasbro on a Star Trek KRE-O animation.

What influences your films and where do your ideas come from?

I'm influenced mostly by what makes me laugh. If I think of an idea that genuinely makes me laugh out loud then it will have a good chance of becoming an animation. Growing up, I watched a lot of movies. Not just American movies but a lot of Asian films, too. Ironically, I was never really a fan of animation or animated movies, but I think my genuine love of film has always been my biggest influence.

The concept for *LEGO Iron Man's New Suit* was inspired by a scene from *Iron Man 3*, correct?

Yes. One of the aspects of the film involved pieces of Iron Man's suit flying toward Tony Stark's body and colliding with it in order to assemble the entire suit around him. I thought it would be funny to make an animation which would depict a more realistic outcome if that were to actually happen.

What planning went into the production?

This animation is driven more by the action than the dialogue, so writing the script mainly involved outlining what happens and when and at which points the main character yells out in pain and why.

Every shot was storyboarded and numbered. My storyboards are usually very simple. I draw basic stick-figure type people to represent the characters and I have a brief outline under each storyboard explaining camera angle, camera position, camera movement, and dialogue.

The set was built in a way that made it easy for me to take apart the walls for any camera angle/position I wanted. I also rigged up some LED lights to illuminate the Iron Man suits in the background, giving the set a more dynamic look.

Lighting and visual effects create atmosphere and action in Keshen8's *Iron Man* spoof.
© Keshen8

© Keshen8

How did you animate all the flying objects?

I used a lot of blue screen (aka green screen or chroma keying). I've never done that before to this extent and I was very pleased with the result. The trick is to blend the blue screened object seamlessly into the shot and one of the ways of doing that effectively, for me, is blue screening the object under the same lighting as everything else.

There are some great sound effects in this movie. What software do you use to create them?

For me, adding sound involves two programs, my editing program (Adobe Premiere Pro) and Pro Tools. Sometimes I will do all of the sound design in Pro Tools but a lot of the time it's used only to edit or add effects to a certain voice or sound. The latter is the case for this animation as most of the sound design was done right in Adobe Premiere Pro.

© Keshen8

What would be your advice to new animators wanting to get their films seen online?

I would say be honest and make what you want to make. Don't try to impress anyone but yourself and have fun. If your stuff is good, people will find it.

LEGO Iron Man's New Suit **was shot using a Canon 7D with 50mm macro lens. Keshen8 uses Adobe Premiere Pro, After Effects, and Dragonframe. To see more of his excellent work go to www.youtube .com/user/Keshen8.**

LIGHTING FOR DRAMA

When you start animating, you're probably going to want to stick to one basic lighting approach. But you'll soon realize that adjusting the lighting, even in a small way, can make a huge difference to the feel of a scene. If you want to incorporate different locations into your film, different times of day, or different moods, you are definitely going to want to change the lighting to reflect that. Lighting is an essential component in injecting drama and helping to tell the story, so it's important to learn how to achieve this. As with

Follow the steps below to achieve the setup shown in the picture for a typical daytime scene.

1. You will need three similar sized lights; the largest you can find will offer the widest distribution of light.
2. Position one of the lights high up to the rear left of your set, directing the light toward a reflector on the opposite right position.
3. Position the second light in the opposite position (the rear right of the set), directing the light toward a reflector on the opposite left position.
4. If you choose to use a third light, attach a sturdy reflector—white card or polystyrene works best—above the set, like a roof, angling it slightly away from you.
5. Position the third light so it's angled upward toward the reflector, but away from your table and set.
6. This should create a flatly, evenly lit set where everything is clearly visible with no heavy shadows. There should be no lamps pointing directly at the set or into your eyes when you are animating. Your set should be loosely boxed in by the lights and reflectors.

RIM LIGHT

FILL LIGHT

BACKGROUND LIGHT

all elements of stop-motion animation, experimentation is key to discovering effects that will work well for your films, but here are the basic types of creative lighting to help you familiarize yourself with the possibilities.

Ambient light

This refers to a consistent light across the whole set, to create the effect of daylight or a well-lit room. An ambient light setup involves the use of reflectors, as described earlier, bouncing the light from two or three sources onto the set.

Rim light

This is a small, focused direct light (used with some diffusion), which is positioned to the rear of the object, sometimes to the rear left or right; the beam of light brushes past the object illuminating the "rim," such as a minifigure's shoulders and hair. Rim lighting (sometimes referred to as back lighting) can be used on its own for dramatic effect, creating a halo around the object, or in combination with a fill light (see below) to bring out extra details in your focused object, adding depth and quality to the image.

Fill light

A fill light is similar to the ambient lighting described previously, but refers to when shooting a particular object or character as opposed to lighting the set itself. You might be retaining the ambient lighting of your daytime scene or using the fill light as your main source of light in a night-time scene, but it is the soft, flat light that helps to illuminate the primary object directly. As with your ambient lights, the fill light should either be diffused or bounced toward a reflector, which in turn illuminates the object.

Background light

For scenes where ambient light is low, it might be a good idea to include a background light; simply put, a light that illuminates the backdrop of your scene, behind the subject. When combined with a fill light and a rim light, this will help to illuminate your subject by reducing any shadows on the back wall created by the other lights. This combination is fairly common for close-up shots of characters.

A spotlight can be used for dramatic effect.
© Jonathan Vaughan

Spotlight

Unlike the other lights described, a spotlight is a tightly focused light pointed directly at a subject as opposed to being diffused or bounced off

Here are some examples of lighting being used to create mood and atmosphere in a variety of Jonathan Vaughan's films.
© Jonathan Vaughan

a reflector. This places a strong focus on the particular object or character. You might want to use a spotlight for a particular naturalistic effect—for example, the light from a helicopter or the headlights from a car, or for more stylized films to create an artificial ambience. Using direct lights, especially on a plastic subject like LEGO, should be used thoughtfully, and probably sparingly too.

Diegetic light

This refers to the source of the light if it is light existing in the world of the film as part of the narrative, for example the glow from a fire or a streetlight. In a live-action film, diegetic light will usually be easily and naturally incorporated, but in stop-motion animation, these are working lights you can incorporate into your set so that it might essentially light itself. Using real lights in your film can enrich it with realism and will help to project a certain level of quality if done well. Here are some tips and ideas for adding diegetic light:

- Electronic elements produced by LEGO, designed to work seamlessly with LEGO toys, are a simple way to add lighting. You have the option of the older 9V Light & Sound System from the 1980s and 1990s if you still have them (or you may buy old sets online), or you can use the more readily available Power Functions products, which were launched in 2008 and are still sold by LEGO. There are also a number of other electronic LEGO products, such as minifigure torches and the LEGO Star Wars LED lightsabers.

- If you're looking for a wider range of lighting options, you might want to try Life-lites, which make micro lighting kits and accessories specifically designed for lighting LEGO models and other scale models.

- Using other LED or fiber-optic devices that you already have, or infrared beams to recreate lasers for a sci-fi battle.

- To create the impression of illuminated LEGO, you can point small focused lights at transparent LEGO pieces. If you don't have a small focused beam (such as a Dedolight with doors on) try creating a pinhole cover filter for a flashlight or LED light that you do have. Rest a wall of transparent bricks on a light box or position a light at one end of a transparent pole to create some really exciting and colorful light effects.

- Why not have a go at building your whole set on top of a light box? This makes a great addition to a disco scene or sci-fi environment. You can buy light boxes fairly cheaply from office supply stores, but you can also create one by positioning an LED light source underneath a supported sheet of frosted Perspex. Check out your local sign making store for cheap (sometimes free!) Perspex off-cuts in a variety of colors.

- You can also use your own laptop screen as a light source, but be sure to make a note of the brightness setting and turn off the power-saving mode, which could affect the light during shooting.

- Lighting effects like these don't have to be difficult. Sometimes even a well-positioned piece of reflector paper can act as an effect light. Try photographing a minifigure seated at a computer screen. Place the white paper on the side of the monitor away from you and the paper will illuminate the minifigure's face just like a screen would. Take some time to think up other ways you can create mood and communicate action using simple techniques like this and it will help to set your film apart.

For his film *CON*, Christian Colglazier created the moody city scene by placing a strand of LED lights in the background, and set the color to blue. "I have a really nice lens for my DSLR which allows for really pretty bokeh," says Christian. "Bokeh is an aesthetic blur caused by out of focus light. I set the camera to a low aperture and it created some really nice backgrounds."
© Christian Colglazier

ADVANCED LIGHTING

Once you've mastered the basics of lighting your set and are feeling more confident, you might be wondering how else you can use lighting to enhance your productions. If you haven't already, you will need to invest in a more professional setup to achieve the next level of results, as household lighting options will always be limiting to an extent. Before you go spending a small fortune on fancy new gear, it's important that you understand the relationship between photographic "depth of field" and the amount of light in your scene, as this is the determining factor that dictates the kind of equipment you will need.

Understanding depth of field

Depth of field refers to the range, or "depth," of your focal area—how much of the image is in focus and how quickly or gradually that focus fades away. A large depth of field or deep focus, where most of the image is sharp, will encourage the viewer to watch what is happening in both the foreground and the background, while a small depth of field or shallow focus allows you to draw the viewer's attention to one particular point or

character in your scene, while de-emphasizing the rest of the image. This focus could be as small as a raised minifigure hand.

A small depth of field draws the eyes to the focused part of the image, in this case a mummified Mexican reveller.
© Paul Hollingsworth

Depth of field in storytelling

Filmmakers have harnessed the technique of depth of field to recreate what our eyes do naturally. Hold your hand up in front of your face and look at it. Now, keeping your hand there, look at the rest of the room. Notice how effortlessly your eyes shift focus. Depth of field is something that we've become accustomed to seeing on the screen, and it is used subtly and sometimes quite pointedly to inform the viewer and tell the story. While it's not necessary to use this in your animation, for an audience to appreciate the characters and setting as "real," it's important to consider where you can use it effectively.

One of the great things about LEGO, which makes it possible for so many people to use it as an animation tool, is its scale—small enough that you can fit your entire set on your desk, and large enough that you can manipulate the arms and legs of your minifigure characters. Of course, that means that your depth of field has to be scaled down too. However, the focal arrangement available to you is very slight as your camera is the same one you might ordinarily use to photograph two humans standing several feet apart, rather than two minifigures with only a couple of inches between them. This can mean that your LEGO photographs can be left looking tellingly model-like—our brains automatically reading the small focal range and telling us that the image depicted is of

These frames from Chris Salt's *Bowling for Sandercoe* and *The Good Life on Mars* use a small depth of field, with a shallow focus.
© Chris Salt

These frames from Chris Salt's *My Dream Train* and *Brick It* show a greater depth of field, with deeper focus.
© Chris Salt

This is the same frame as seen on page 66 but with the aperture closed. There is greater focal depth and more of the characters are in focus, but the image is prohibitively dark because no other settings have been changed.
© Paul Hollingsworth

Here is the same shot again, but because of longer exposure settings, the scene is now visible.
© Paul Hollingsworth

By introducing stronger lighting, you can appreciate more of the image's detail.
© Paul Hollingsworth

something tiny. Luckily, there are two techniques we can employ to help these images to look more life-size and to bring the audience into the world of the minifigure.

Depth of field in relation to aperture

Hold a small image up close to your face, and notice how you need to narrow your eyes to focus on it. This is a good way to think of aperture in relation to depth of field. By narrowing the aperture on your camera (done by increasing the f-number), you can get up close to your minifigures, making it easier to create cinematic compositions in your LEGO world. When this happens, the amount of light that reaches the sensor is decreased, so while you now have the best depth of field you won't be able to see the image properly, because it is so dark. You could take the photographs using a longer exposure, as explained earlier, but this will only affect the photographic frames and not the live video feed you are using to determine each shot, essentially your workspace. A better option is to opt for stronger, more powerful lights—hence why you always see these kinds of lights on professional film sets.

For many readers, venturing into the expensive world of professional lighting will be a big financial investment, so think about how much an advanced lighting setup will improve the overall look of your films and how important it is to you to achieve that level of quality before purchasing any new equipment.

For those wanting to take a smaller step in this direction, a more affordable and elegant midway solution is the use of LED panels. These can be left on for long periods of time without overheating; they remain cool to touch and are much lighter than their tungsten equivalents making them easy to handle, and they produce an attractive, even body of white light.

The next rung on the ladder will take you to basic professional lighting with the purchase of a Dedo Kit—a ready-to-use kit manufactured by Dedolight. A good choice for a beginner would be a basic three 150W light kit, which comes with light stands, directional shutters, and everything that you will need to use them. Beyond that, you're looking at purchasing studio lights—a subject for a whole other book.

TOP TIP—CHEAP CHEAT

"If you can't afford brighter lights, but you're still having problems capturing your desired exposures while also seeing the live view, an alternative solution is to use a second camera entirely for your animation window," says Tony Mines. "This could be a simple webcam or other device positioned next to or near the main camera that's capturing the longer-exposure photographs. While it will never precisely match the angle, it will allow you to follow the process of your animation with something roughly similar."

PREPARING YOUR STUDIO

4

The space you choose to animate in, known as your studio, might be your bedroom, a spare room in your house, a garage, basement, or even a purpose-built studio space, if you're lucky. Wherever it is, this space is where you will spend a lot of time while working on your films, so it's imperative that it meets the criteria set out in this chapter in order to give your productions a solid foundation. In animation, the animator is the actor, acting through the characters and objects. We can look at preparing your studio space as akin to an actor getting ready to perform. Having the space set up correctly allows you to get into character and focus on animating.

You might have thought animation was all about moving things, but it's probably more important that you master the art of keeping everything still. If you are animating a minifigure's arm, that arm and you should be the only things to move. The camera, the table, the lights, the set, and everything else on it should remain motionless. When you're shooting LEGO, the scale is unforgiving when it comes to unwanted miniscule movements. If the wrong thing unexpectedly moves during your shoot, you could set yourself back hours, and it can be very frustrating and demoralizing, not just for beginners.

This is the stage in the animating process where you step into the shiny plastic skin of a LEGO minifigure—essentially seeing the world from a 1.5-inch-tall perspective. Observing the world this way will help you avoid obvious pitfalls and foolproof your sets and studio space.

CHOOSING YOUR ROOM

No one is expecting you to go out and start renting a professional photography studio to make your LEGO films—most amateurs and some professionals animate from a room in their own home. Depending on where you live, you might need to do some rearranging to accommodate your new hobby, or borrow a space from a friend or family member if your own home is not appropriate. A room that comprises the conditions that follow would be most suitable.

- Size—the size of the room might determine the work surface you can fit in it and the scale of films you can make. For beginners this probably won't be a big concern as most rooms should be able to accommodate

© Paul Hollingsworth

a usable work surface, computer, lights, and camera, but if the room serves more than one purpose (e.g., a spare bedroom) think about how the furniture can be arranged to maximize the animating space and to avoid your equipment being disturbed.

- No natural light—it is quite rare for a room to have no natural light, which is why basements are popular choices for animators. A basement or windowless room might not be available to you, so blackout blinds, curtains, and black tape to seal up any unwanted slivers of light are alternative options. Remember to seal up any crack of light from doorways too.
- Dark walls—this will help prevent any unwanted light reflections bouncing off the walls onto your set. If you're dedicating a room to your animating, it might be worth painting the walls.
- Ground floor or basement with a concrete floor—uneven floorboards might make it quite hard to create a truly flat surface for your set and small movements might be caused by you walking around the set. An even concrete floor on ground level will provide you with a reliable, solid surface to put your table and equipment on.
- Multiple plug points—as you now know, there are a number of electrical elements that are required for a production, and having easy access to a number of plug sockets will make your studio safe and simple to navigate around.

David Boddy's studio space with overhead light.
© David Boddy

Inside My Studio: David Boddy

"Downstairs at my house the garage has been converted to a rumpus room, which is a sea of loose LEGO bricks and my custom LEGO creations. Adjoining this room is a bit of a tool shed. I've blacked out the one window in there, set up an overhead light source and a table to record on. I started initially with a video camera and then switched to using a Logitech webcam to record. They are cheap and produce really good results. I've recently purchased a DSLR and am slowly teaching myself the complexity of digital photography."

CHOOSING YOUR WORK SURFACE

The surface you animate on is equally important as the room you choose. There's no point spending hours building a beautifully detailed set only to find that the table you built it on lets down the overall look of the film. Here are the main points to look out for.

- Height—as you are most likely to be standing while you animate, your table or surface should be at a suitable height for you, where you can reach over the whole set comfortably without having to bend over.
- Surface area—the table needs to be able to accommodate the sets you want to shoot with room to spare for fixing lights. It's better to have a bit more space than you need rather than trying to squeeze everything onto a small table.

- Sturdiness—this is possibly the most important factor to consider. A good way to assess the table for this is to stand a minifigure on it and take your eyes down to its eye level. Gently nudge the table and see how much it wobbles, or lean on the surface slightly and look at how much it compresses. If there's even a small movement—or worse, the minifigure topples over—the table is probably not suitable. A few fractions of an inch of movement scaled up is more like a foot to a minifigure! Try choosing a table made from a thick heavy wood, or one with cross brackets on the legs. A box-shaped desk with sides, a large chest of drawers, or a work surface that's firmly secured to a wall can all be good solid options.

Choose a sturdy wooden table with thick legs that won't cause your set to wobble or move.
© Paul Hollingsworth

Paul Hollingsworth animating in his converted studio space.
© Paul Hollingsworth

Inside My Studio: Paul Hollingsworth

"I've shot in whatever space I could use from my kitchen, living room, storage space, and a friend's garage. We recently moved to a house in LA and I converted my garage to a studio. There's a lot of shelf space for LEGO models and drawers to keep bricks sorted, tables for building, and a table for the main set. I like having everything at my fingertips. When I'm in the creative zone I just want to build so all LEGO bricks, plates, tiles, slopes, and minifigs have been sorted. Organization is key. I also have a backdrop for chroma keying, and there's tons of space for my nine-foot motion control rig. That is my pride and joy."

TRIPODS

Most stop-motion animation is produced using a tripod, as keeping the camera completely still is one of the primary requirements for the medium to work. Any kind of tripod should be able to keep your camera steady, but with varying degrees of ease and efficiency. A good quality model with as few loose parts as possible is ideal. Your tripod will have a varying number of knobs and dials to alter the height of your camera. It might also have an air bubble feature that you can use to make sure the camera plate is sitting level. Once you've found a position you're happy with, make sure you lock everything in place as tightly as possible. If you're looking to create more elaborate panning or tilted shots, you'll need a tripod with a geared head, although shooting LEGO offers some clever alternatives to physically moving the camera (see "moving the camera" on page 132).

To stop your tripod from toppling over, or shifting slightly, it's advisable to fix it to the floor. Concrete or tiled floors are best for this as you can use stick putty underneath each tripod foot or duct tape. You can also buy spreaders to attach to your tripod's feet that can be anchored down with sandbags. If you want a more permanent solution, you could screw or nail the tripod down. If it's not possible for you to keep the tripod stationary for the duration of your shoot, then the next best option is to mark the position of each leg of the tripod on the floor with colored sticky tape. That way you'll know precisely where to reinstall it. If you're using a webcam or other camera that does not allow you to dock it to a tripod, then you can build a small rig out of LEGO, which can then be connected to LEGO baseplates for stability.

Examples of LEGO rigs built around webcams by David Boddy (left) and Zach Boivin (right). These cameras can be attached directly to the set for stability.
© David Boddy © Zach Boivin

Inside My Studio: Chris Salt

"My 'studio' is the desk where my computer is. There's a space next to the monitor that can fit a couple of LEGO baseplates and that's where everything happens. I started out with the equipment I had on hand—a webcam, some desk lamps, and a box of childhood LEGO complete with bite marks and mysterious stains. Over time I upgraded all that, trying out different cameras, buying some proper photographic lights, and buying quite a lot more LEGO. The amount of space around the desk has steadily reduced over the years as the LEGO collection has grown."

A look inside Chris Salt's studio while he was filming *Jane's Brain*.
© Chris Salt

HOW TO TURN YOUR ROOM INTO A STUDIO

With a suitable room and work surface selected, you are ready to transform that space into your studio. If the room does have windows, block out all the natural light if you can. If the room is one used for multiple purposes, consider investing in blackout blinds and heavy curtains, so it's quicker and easier to transform the space. If for any reason you are unable to block out the light, it might be best to consider animating only at nighttime.

Make sure the floor is as flat and even as possible, especially important if you have to use a room with wooden floorboards or an uneven floor covering. If the floor you're using is particularly springy, then when you walk near your camera or work surface, there is a chance you could accidentally shift the position of either. Rearrange the furniture if need be so there is ample space around the work surface for you to access all of your set. Fix your main lighting setup in place and consider installing a shelf or surface high above your work surface for any hanging attachments, or aerial lighting setups you might want to use. Ensure your work surface is secure and tape down any cables from your computer, camera, or lights that are likely to be a safety risk. It's also a good idea to fix your set in place, using Blu-Tack or another removable adhesive.

Set-building tips

Building your first LEGO movie set can be a fun experience, but it's a good idea to keep the following things in mind:

Once you've decided on a room and a work surface, set the space up in the way that you think works best based on the tips mentioned previously. Move the furniture if necessary. Set up your camera on a tripod and think about how you will use the space when you're animating, so you can troubleshoot for any potential problems.

- *It's a small world*—It can be tempting to go all out and spend days and weeks building an elaborate MOC to feature as the backdrop for your first LEGO movie, but it's best to start off small. If you're animating for the first time, you probably want to get on with making the film rather than devoting your time to constructing the set, which leads to the next point . . .

- *What will you see?*—Unlike an imaginative MOC, which you can photograph from every angle to showcase online, a relatively small amount of your set might be on display in your film. If you're planning on lots of character close-ups, then that intricate cheese-slope mosaic floor might never be seen by the camera. By storyboarding in advance you can figure out exactly what you need to

TOP TIP—SEE IT, BUILD IT

"A general rule I try to follow is to only build what the camera will see," says Chris Salt. "It's easy to get carried away playing with the LEGO and building an awesome model only to find, when you come to film it, that it's way too big to fit in a shot. Often, I'll point the camera at a character and then build a set around them in order to make sure everything that needs to be there fits in the frame."

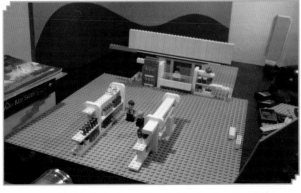

While the finished shot on the right creates the illusion of an entire supermarket, the behind-the-scenes image reveals what Chris Salt actually built for this scene in Jane's Brain.
© Chris Salt

build and what you can leave to the audience's imagination.

- *Build it in situ*—This is important especially if your film does require a larger, more complex set that's hard to transport. Building in front of the camera will also help you to determine how the set is coming along and how it looks under the lights.

- *Access all areas*—When you're building, think about your characters, where they will be in the scene, and how you are going to access them to animate. This might require you to build an easily removable wall or to make sure your background props are secured in place.

READY TO SHOOT!

With your studio set up, your lighting arranged, and your sets built, it's time to start animating! Make sure your studio is ready to go with this checklist.

- [ ] Studio is blacked out
- [ ] Floor is even
- [ ] Workspace is solid and flat
- [ ] Cables are taped down
- [ ] Room to stand away from the set
- [ ] Lights are positioned correctly
- [ ] Diffusers are a safe distance from the lights
- [ ] Reflectors are in position
- [ ] Camera is secured to a tripod
- [ ] You're dressed in dark colored clothing
- [ ] Set is accessible

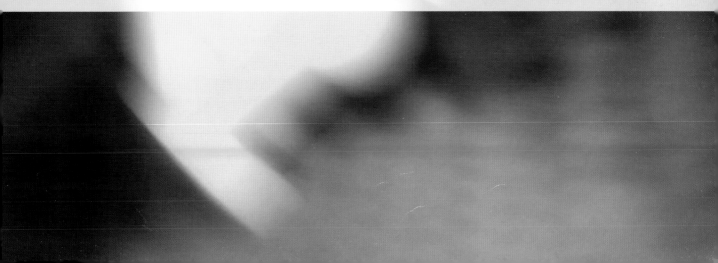

5

HOW TO ANIMATE

"The way I look at animating is that there is no one right way to do something," says Daniel Utecht. "There are always multiple ways to accomplish a task and it's up to each individual animator to decide what's best. Animating is great because it involves lots of imagination, creativity, and freedom. We live in a relatively structured world so it's relaxing to have an activity that allows for as much structure and order or chaos and disorder as we see fit." In this chapter we will be exploring some of the ways you can use LEGO to make stop-motion films, and some of the ways to achieve certain effects. This should set you up to start exploring your own ways of making movie magic.

DIFFERENT WAYS TO ANIMATE WITH LEGO

While constructing models with LEGO bricks might seem restrictive at first, it is the very "rules" that seem to limit the possibilities that encourage hobbyists to push boundaries and come up with ingenious ways to build with the diverse array of bricks and parts. This creative liberation is abundant in the LEGO film community too, and arguably the ability to add sound, music, and special effects make LEGO animations all the more diverse.

While there are a number of ways to use LEGO toys for stop-motion animation, there is one popular style that dominates forums and YouTube channels—character animation using minifigures. Despite often being referred to as "brick-films," these movies don't usually involve much animation of LEGO *bricks*, but rather of the delightful minifigure population of the LEGO world. And it's not hard to see why. LEGO minifigures make the ideal subjects for those starting out on their animation journey, and for more experienced animators, they provide a scaled-down universe of mathematical precision to do with as they will.

This chapter will cover the ways in which you can use stop-motion animation to bring your minifigure collection to life, but it will also offer some alternative ways to combine LEGO with animation that you might not have thought of or seen before. Applying the same techniques to larger models, original MOCs of robots or monsters, or to your other LEGO Bionicle figures brings a whole new dimension to your films. We'll also explore replacement or sequential animation—building models or patterns that change with time—and animating collage pictures or patterns with flat LEGO tiles or walls of bricks to bring them to life. And for those of you wanting to take things back to basics, live video techniques that don't involve any animation are another great way to incorporate LEGO into films. All these techniques can be used separately or in conjunction with each other to great effect.

HOW TO ANIMATE LIKE A PRO, IN TWO EASY STEPS!

While animating LEGO comes with its own particular tricks and challenges, most of what you'll need to know to get started can be applied universally to stop-motion animation. Animation is about creating movement, and quality animation is about making that movement smooth and believable. Below are two easy tips, which, used separately or combined, will noticeably improve any animation tenfold, whether you're using minifigures, clay models, drawings, or CG creations. Characters or clouds, special effects or title texts, all will move like they do in the movies if you just remember these things:

1. Easing
2. Rebound and anticipation

Easing

Animation is about tricking the eye into believing that something is moving on its own and sometimes the way to trick the eye is to build expectation. When you animate a simple movement, say the sudden raising of an arm, even if you want the overall movement to be fast, you should "ease"

into the movement by making the change in the first few frames slighter, then increase gradually. This lets the eye subconsciously register that the arm is set to move, and helps the viewer receive the overall action as "smooth." To move the arm suddenly and evenly, without easing, would result in a "jerky" movement (though this might be desirable if you are animating a robot, or a sudden exclamation of a character).

Of course, if you "ease out" of the move as well as "ease in," the move will appear more fluid than if you came to a sudden stop. Easing also helps the eye to follow complex actions, if a set of two or more moves are set to follow in quick succession.

Rebound and anticipation

To understand the principle of rebound, try this quick test. Facing forward, try to raise your own hand very suddenly ahead of your view, such as it comes to an absolute and sudden stop. Can't quite do it, can you? No matter how hard you try to make it stop dead, it will always bounce a little, moving down a touch, then back up again. This is because very little in real life can come to an absolute and sudden stop, like it might in a computer

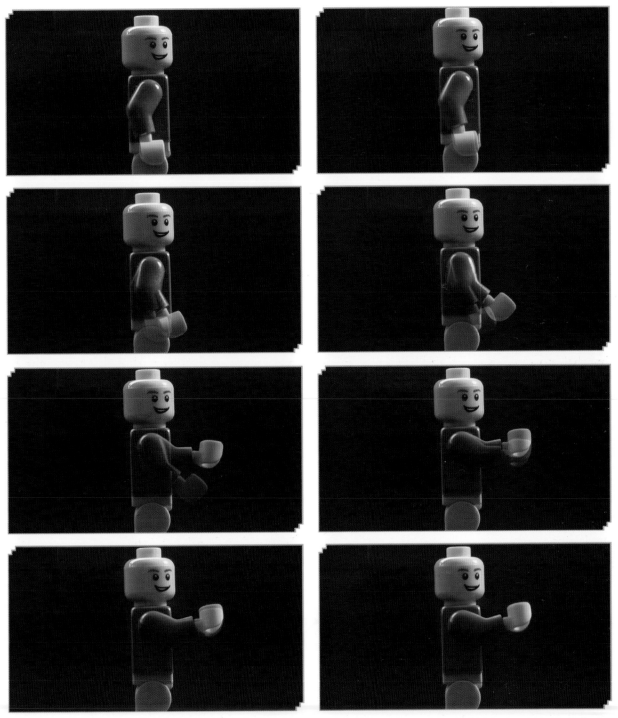

This sequence shows easing in and easing out applied to the action of raising an arm. Note how the first and last movements are incrementally smaller than the movements in the middle of the action.
© Jordan Johnson

The best way to get the hang of this technique is to experiment with different speeds of easing and not easing, and note the effects each attempt creates. With this technique alone you can convey different ideas of weight and even different expressions of mood. Try shooting a minifigure raising its arm, or slamming its arm down. Adjust the easing to create different effects.

simulation. This is the principle of rebound, or bounce.

Applying this to your animations is simple. When you come to the end of a move, if an arm is moving up to a position, have it shift back down from the end pose for a frame or two before coming to a stop. Or have it shift back down, then bounce back up again to its end pose. If you want a car to move forward and then come to a sudden stop, have it bounce back a touch, then settle forward to a stop. The opposite of rebound is *anticipation*. Anticipation is when you "rev" into a move with an "anticipatory" shift in the reverse direction: a slight move to the left before moving right, or a slight move down before moving up. Like easing, anticipation frames help the eye subconsciously prepare for a move, while relaying particular ideas about weight and physics. Many simple moves can be aided with just a subtle, single anticipation frame. But equally, an anticipation move might be a whole action of its own, like a crouch in preparation for a leap. You might decide never to make your minifigures fly through the air or add in visual effects of explosions, but if you can manage to apply these simple techniques, you'll be animating like a pro in no time!

As with easing, experimentation is the best way to establish the effects of different scales of rebound. Try the arm move again or film a LEGO car braking. Most moves require only the subtlest hint, perhaps a frame or two, and be careful not to overdo it as too much bounce on each move can make everything look like elastic. Again, different implementations will suggest different weights, materials, and levels of force.

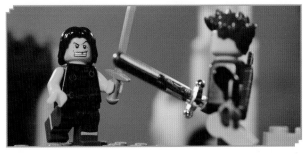

By lowering the sword slightly in the final image of the sequence, natural rebound movement is simulated.
© Paul Hollingsworth

Anticipation of the raised sword action is created by the slight lowering of the arm and leg swinging backward in the second frame, before the launch into the raised sword of the third frame.
© Paul Hollingsworth

HOW TO ANIMATE

93

Another example of anticipation being used to create a realistic motion—notice how the minifigure's arms are thrown back first and then forward into the jump.
© Paul Hollingsworth

UNDERSTANDING FRAME RATE

A commonly discussed question on stop-motion forums, especially among those just starting out, is: what frame rate should I be using? First, let's clear up what a frame rate actually is, for those new to the expression. Quite simply, the frame rate refers to the frequency that sequential images are displayed on a television, in a film, or in a video. A principle, known as the "phi phenomenon," explains how our brains naturally process a sequence of still images or frames as depicting movement, so long as the frames are shown at a particular speed. If the speed is too slow then the principle fails and our brains can detect the individual images, but with enough images per second, we are able to see movement.

While there are certain agreed upon standards that have endured, there is no universally "correct" frame rate that you have to use. One of the more common choices is 25 frames per second (fps). The reason being is that 25 is a good number to work with. It's easy to remember that for four seconds of video you will need 100 frames, or for ten seconds of video you will need 250 frames. When you're shooting your films it makes it quicker to calculate how far along you are.

However, if you're thinking that photographing 100 frames for only four seconds of video seems like a bit more work than you'd bargained for, you can choose to animate "on twos"—a phrase used to describe the process of using two identical images for each frame. In short, this approach halves the amount of animation work you have to do to fill a second by shooting fifty different frames and using each one twice, to equal 100 frames, filling four seconds more quickly. If you do decide to do this, it might be better to shoot at 24fps, because it's an even number and that way you know you only need twelve different shots, used twice each, for each second.

Setting your software to capture at 24fps is preferable to shooting at 12fps, because this gives you the flexibility to shoot some scenes on twos and revert to shooting "on ones" for faster actions, as shooting on twos might be too slow to show the action effectively and fluidly. While 25fps is preferable, your frame rate decision will depend on what kind of action you're shooting, the speed at which you would like to animate, and how smooth you would like your animation sequences to look.

Combining live video and stop-motion frame rates

If you're combining live video and stop-motion, you will need to match the frame rates of both sequences for a more seamless transition. You might be shooting some footage of yourself smashing a LEGO city to smithereens and then cut to stop-motion footage of your minifigure characters running away. In this instance, you should animate the stop-motion sequences using your camera's "native" frame rate for video footage. This will vary from camera model to camera model, and will be determined by the type of camera and the country of origin.

Export frame rate

Separate to the question of animation frame rate is "export frame rate." This refers to the frame rate settings you use to export your finished film, either to upload to the Internet or onto DVD. If you're exporting to the Internet, then you should be able to export using whichever frame rate you've animated your video in, whereas if you're exporting for television viewing or for DVD, your settings will vary depending on where you are in the world, and you should use the format and settings you would normally use to export nonanimated video. Remember, this doesn't affect the frame rate that you animate at. Your software's video export function will correctly interpret any difference.

How to Avoid Problems in the Studio

- *Watch yourself*—You've probably thought to look out for your hands sneaking into shots where they're not wanted, but it's not just your hands you need to be wary of. Look out for any shadows your body is casting on the sets and characters, or any light that is bouncing off your clothes or skin; our skin can reflect a surprising amount of light.

- *Dress for the occasion*—Because of unwanted reflections, it's a good idea to wear dark colors, covering most of your body.

- *Step away*—When it's time to take a frame, don't just lean back from the set, but take a big step away to avoid casting a shadow or affecting the light in any way. You might not see it immediately, but if you're too close to the set you will start to notice the light bouncing around in your shots. A good technique is to choose a "safe spot" marked on the floor or with a chair where you can comfortably retreat to knowing it won't affect your lighting.

- *Take a second*—When you move away from the set, give everything a few seconds to settle into place before taking the shot. This is especially important if you've applied pressure to the table, the set, or the character you're filming. They might all need a second to reset to their natural state. These movements might not be seen by the naked eye, but could be picked up on your camera, so it's worth taking the extra time for a better finish.

- *No pressure*—In light of the last tip, it's a good idea to avoid putting pressure on the table or work surface directly. This is one of the reasons for recommending a surface that is just above waist height, so you don't have to bend over too much to make adjustments or reach up onto a higher table.

- *Limber up*—Before you start animating a piece or minifigure, it's a good idea to play around with it, testing all the joints to make sure they're not sticking. Older joints can become loose, so watch out for these parts too.

- *And that goes for you too*—Animating means long hours standing, concentrating, and moving things by very small amounts. If you don't take regular breaks and keep your body hydrated, fed, and well-stretched, you will start to feel tired and uncomfortable, and this will lead to mistakes.

- *Time-out*—If you do take a break, especially if you're midway through filming a sequence, thoroughly assess the set when you return to make sure nothing has moved in your absence, and that the heat of the lights hasn't warped your table or any of the LEGO.

HOW TO ANIMATE

SILHOUETTES

Maximize your minifigures' limited body movements by creating strong, dynamic shapes.
© Paul Hollingsworth

Earlier, we mentioned the phi phenomenon—how our brains interpret a sequence of still images as a moving image. For this principle to work, not only do the images have to be shown in a fast enough frame rate, but the images have to relate to each other—the subjects creating clear, confident shapes to direct the viewer's attention and convey the story. This overall idea of creating shapes in animation is referred to as silhouettes.

Silhouettes are what bring characters to life. As cute and colorful as they are, minifigures are far from their human equivalents in terms of movability, flexibility, and expression. As with all stop-motion models, the animator must inject character into these inanimate objects to bring them to life on screen. Minifigures have their limitations—they don't have knees, fingers, or moving facial features, and their arms only rotate on a single axis. Some animators harness these limitations and use them to great comedic affect, together with other characteristics, like the minifigure's ability to turn its head round 360 degrees. Strong silhouettes—or the overall space that the character is occupying—are necessary for the audience to understand the minifigure in all its simplicity.

Like easing and rebound, this fundamental animation technique is developed from drawn animation, and will help to get the most life out of your minifigure characters. Before you start shooting your scene, look at the minifigures in it and think about the shapes that their bodies are making. Are they just a group of square guys standing around, or is there an obvious focus to the scene? If there is a focus—a minifigure brandishing a sword raised to the sky, for example—how are the other characters' bodies responding to that focus and what does it tell us about what's happening? Can we tell if the other characters are scared or excited from their poses? Does the silhouette of the image convey meaning

Now that you've learned about all the fundamental techniques of animation, why not try combining them in practice, using a simple selection of bricks. See if you can turn a set of slopes and blocks into believable blob-monsters, using anticipation, rebound, and strong silhouettes.

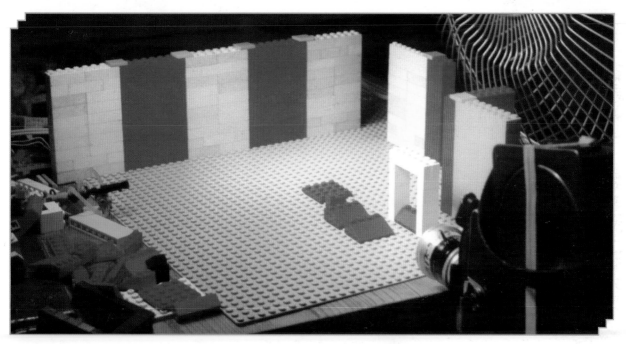

Sloped bricks as blob monsters in Lindsay Fleay's *The Magic Portal*.
© Lindsay Fleay

without script, sound, or the preceding or following images? If yes, then you're on the right track. This shape should change and shift as the scene progresses, pulling the audience's focus as it does so.

If you film a minifigure moving from one side of the screen to the other fairly quickly, the audience will infer that he ran there, but they won't *feel* that he did. If he throws his arms back in anticipation at the start of the run, then throws his arms up at the end, these poses will convey the energy of the movement, instilling a confidence in the audience that he did in fact run from one side to the other.

SECONDARY MOVEMENT

Without secondary movement, it's not obvious that this minifigure is about to throw the hammer.
© Paul Hollingsworth

An important and rather simple technique to consider when animating minifigures is to use your own body to perform the movements you want your minifigure to replicate. The LEGO population might not be blessed with our human flexibility and number of joints, but by using secondary movements you can increase the realistic appearance of your characters. A secondary movement is something you will animate to make the audience believe in the primary movement, similar to rebound. For example, try mimicking the action of throwing a ball. It's not just your throwing arm that moves, is it? Maybe your body twists slightly, or you shift the weight on your feet. Maybe your other arm moves backward for balance or your turn your head slightly. These are all secondary movements that you could incorporate into your animation. While a raised and lowered arm throwing a ball would be enough to let the audience know what has occurred, these additional movements will sell the idea that the minifigure has a connected anatomy. These movements are particularly useful when trying to create the illusion of weight or force.

By including secondary movements, the hammer looks heavier and the force of the throw is more apparent.
© Paul Hollingsworth

Come up with some of your own ways to practice secondary movement, and see how it brings your animation to life. Use everyday actions that you can model on your own movements to get started. If you're having trouble seeing what the secondary movements to an action are, film yourself first and watch how you move, or ask a friend to help.

WALKING

By understanding and practicing the concepts of silhouettes and secondary movement, you will be well positioned to animate a good minifigure walk—a technique you are almost definitely going to need in your films.

An example of a walk cycle.
© Paul Hollingsworth

A "walk cycle" is the repetitious action you will use to make it look like your minifigure is walking across the set. Each cycle contains two apexes—these are the points where the limbs are at the extreme of their movement (i.e., when the left leg is fully forward with the right arm fully back, and when the right arm is fully forward with the left leg fully back). By alternating the legs and arms this way, it creates a feeling of dexterity and gives the impression that the minifigure has an anatomy similar to a human's, with hips and shoulders moving as it walks. By juxtaposing the arms and legs in this way, it also creates a strong silhouette as the minifigure moves, making it clear to the audience that he is walking.

You can also include two distinct secondary movements. One is the hands turning at the wrist; inward at the beginning of the swing, and then outward at the back, which helps to make the arms look like they are moving fluidly, as a human's would at the elbow. The other is a slight twist of the head at each apex, to one side and then the other. This gives the minifigure a visual spine—a body completely connected from head to toe.

The number of frames in a single walk cycle will depend on you, your character, and the situation. If you have strong alternating poses that help to convey the movement, you can achieve a simple walk cycle with just four frames. But for a more regular walk, you will probably require ten or twelve frames. Shooting twelve frames for each walk cycle, especially if you want your character to walk for a couple of seconds, could add up. It can be hard to keep track of what your minifigure is doing. If you find yourself asking, "Was this leg going forward or backward?" more than you would like, it might be a good idea to make a list of the frames and tick them off as you go so you don't get confused. A crude drawing that shows the frames of the cycle or a simple tally that indicates when the leading leg has reached its apex, should help to keep the process in check.

 Create your own walk cycle. If you're feeling ambitious, experiment with altering the walk slightly to see how it changes the character, or try the walk on a studless surface.

Stud walk: pros and cons

Lots of animators will use a LEGO baseplate when they start animating walking for the first time. This is both helpful and limiting. In the first instance, the studs are a reliable and efficient way of keeping your minifigure upright while walking, and the studs' even spacing keeps your walk cycle regular and even. It also makes it easier to keep track of your progress by counting the studs. What you might not consider, however, are the limitations of using a baseplate. The evenness of the spacing means you are restricted to a very functional, robotic walk. It's a useful technique for conveying a simple stroll or to animate lots of minifigures walking all at once. But if you're looking to achieve more animated walk cycles, then be brave and animate on a smooth surface—not on LEGO at all, or a tiled LEGO baseplate.

An adhesive putty, such as Bostick's Blu-Tack, can be used to secure the feet of minifigures for studless walks. Place a small lump of the putty on the load-bearing heel, then as you move into the next footstep, remove the putty and place a new lump under the opposite foot. A small lump on one foot will be enough to support the whole minifigure. There's no need to worry too much about the putty being visible; you can get away with this in one or two frames because it will quickly disappear again every time the foot is placed. The more realistic the walk, the more the audience will buy into the illusion you're creating, and the less likely they are to notice the use of putty.

Zach Macias of MindGame Studios was introduced to stop-motion ten years ago as a teenager and hasn't put the camera down since. In his film *Stranger than Fishin'* he used studless animation to great effect. Here he explains why he's so proud of the film.

© Zach Macias

When and how were you inspired to start making brick-films?

My history with stop-motion dates back to around 2004, when I was thirteen. My neighbor and I were bored one summer afternoon when he suggested we make a short film to occupy ourselves. It was there that he introduced me to the stop-motion animation technique, hitting the record button on and off as quickly as possible before moving chess pieces along a couple of inches. For many, I can imagine this coming off as fairly tedious, but something about making and watching a short film come to life like that was very compelling to me.

A month or so later, I was browsing Yahoo! when I saw an advertisement for a LEGO *Spider-Man 2*

video, which would turn out to be *Spider-Man: The Peril of Doc Ock* by Spite Your Face Productions. It was my first introduction to stop-motion with LEGO bricks, and I was completely blown away. The quality of the animation, sets, visual effects, and overall production design was so far above and beyond what I even thought was possible, especially with LEGO of all things. I then remembered that I had boxes of LEGO sitting in the back of my closet collecting dust, and I thought to myself, "Hey, maybe I can do something like this." From there, the rest is pretty much history.

You've used simple ideas to great effect, as with *Stranger than Fishin'*—how do you go about planning a short film like that?

Stranger than Fishin' was one of the more interesting projects I've worked on, as far as the planning stage goes. The original concept for this film was meant to be about thirty to forty-five seconds in length and primarily a one-joke story about a fisherman who gets a big bite on

his first cast, but it turns out to be a giant shark and he is abruptly eaten whole when he reels it in. I started work on it over spring break of my freshman year in college.

What were the challenges you faced in terms of shooting the film?

What I initially thought was going to be an easy shoot turned out to be much more time-consuming than I expected, and I was only able to get about a quarter of it done during the break. It's never a good feeling to have to leave a project incomplete, and I was certainly unhappy to at the time, but in this case I believe the film benefitted greatly from the time away. When I came back to it, the idea had vastly evolved and I had a number of ideas for new, more complex animation sequences, and it had become an actual "story" rather than a simple throwaway gag like originally intended. The animation process took about two and a half weeks, and then an additional week for editing/sound design.

Behind the scenes filming *Stranger than Fishin'*.
© Zach Macias

What did that week of editing involve?

One of the benefits of stop-motion is that, if you're keen on your sense of timing, you can usually calculate how long exactly you want each shot to be. In that sense, the editing is almost done for you as you go along; you can just drop your rendered animation sequences in order in your video editor and, save trimming or adding a few frames here or there, it's basically assembled. What I think was the most fascinating part of the video editing stage was the discovery of just how perfectly "The Barber of Seville" overture matched up to it with little to no adjustment. The pacing of the film matched up exactly with the pacing of the music. Music selection is something that I still kind of struggle with, so it's

always nice to have little accidental moments like that where you try something like that and it works out beautifully.

What were you most proud of about the completed film?

I'm most proud of the actual animation. The majority of the film is shot on flat plates as opposed to a surface with the more classical LEGO studs to stick figures on. If there's one thing that LEGO animators can be kind of spoiled with, it's having the studs to keep figures in place, which makes animating them much easier. Without that, you have to rely fairly heavily on some sort of a clay or tack to hold them down, but honestly, I find the absence of the LEGO studs to be a little bit liberating. There's a greater range of mobility that you can achieve on a flat surface over a studded surface if you have the patience and steadiness for it. There's a shot in the film where the protagonist is reeling in a big catch—perhaps my favorite shot in the film. It's a close-up of his feet as he tries to back pedal only to be pulled forward and skid across the dock. It was a really tough shot to pull off, especially when the camera was zoomed in that close. I did my best to hide the clay I used to keep him in place, but you can

still see it if you look closely. I'm very happy with how the animation turned out, and a scene like that would have been nearly impossible to do on a studded surface.

What has been the reaction to the film?

In general, reaction from my subscriber base was very positive. It's among my most-viewed films on my YouTube channel. It has also done well in offline platforms as well—I submitted the film to UCLA's Shorts on the Hill festival and it ended up winning. The film was made nearly four years ago, but I am still of the belief that it's the best thing I've made yet; it's usually the first film that I show to people when I introduce my work to them. I sometimes have trouble watching my own films with other people, but *Stranger* is one that I'm usually proud to show off.

***Stranger than Fishin'* was shot on a Canon HV30. Zach used Dragonframe, Final Cut Pro, Adobe After Effects, and Audacity to make the film. To watch the film and more from Mind-Game Studios and Zach Macias go to www.youtube.com/user/ZachMG.**

Caption: Zach used sticky clay to balance the minifigure in this clever shot.
© Zach Macias

Other walking methods

- If you decide that your scene calls for a closer framing of your minifigure (e.g., the feet are out of shot), you can try pushing the character forward on the end of a thin LEGO plate, balancing on one stud, then alternating each step, moving the plate forward incrementally. Using this kind of method to propel your characters frees you up to create dynamic and gravity-defying poses.

- If the feet are out of the shot, you can also try using a LEGO turntable part, or a combination of a turntable and plate to include a twist in the hips that you can't achieve using a simple walk. If you move the plate gradually forward, and rhythmically rotate the turntable as you go, you'll be able to produce a much smoother, more realistic-looking walk.

ANIMATION ACTING WITH MINIFIGURES

One of the questions professional animators are often asked is: how do you know how many frames to shoot for a particular move? Unfortunately, as with most art forms, the answer to this is intuition. Animators spend hundreds of hours with their characters, learning how to communicate different intentions and emotions, observing human or animal behavior, and trying to instill that into a small clay or plastic model. It's something that takes practice and through trial and error you will come to learn what works for your characters and movements.

Think of animating like acting—an actor will rehearse his lines and movements in his mind and then act it out on the stage or in front of the camera. As you animate, frame by frame, you are acting out this performance through the minifigure. On your first try you may be surprised by how fast your moves are acted out when you see them in sequence, or by how slow they are. Through observing your work and the work of others, you'll soon learn how to adjust the number of frames required in an action to create the look you want.

A few general tips

- As mentioned earlier, limbering up your minifigures is an important phase of the animation process, especially if they're brand new. Just like humans, these little actors will stiffen up if they're left sitting around doing nothing. Do this right before putting the minifigure into the scene, turning all the joints 360 degrees and giving everything a good wiggle. This will avoid the nuisance of filming half of a scene and then discovering your minifigure has a particularly stiff neck.

- Don't scrimp on the sticky stuff; put a firm wedge of Blu-Tack or your putty of choice under hair pieces and hats so that they don't accidentally twist around when you're animating the head. If you're not averse to the permanence of glue, you could use this instead.

- Minifigures are reflective, and not in the soul-searching, thoughtful kind of way. Their faces and shoulders especially are curved and shiny. While a standalone reflection might not be a problem for a photograph, a sequence of photographs with changing reflections will start to be noticeable. All the more reason to take that full step back so a reflection of yourself does not form part of the shot.

- Just like notoriously difficult Hollywood stars, minifigures can be a tricky bunch to work with. Next are some body-part specific tips to make your days on set as stress-free as possible.

Minifigure heads

You might be thinking there isn't much you can do with a minifigure head, as far as animation is concerned. Well, you'd be wrong. Put aside the huge range of minifigure faces and expressions that LEGO makes, and consider the different combinations of speeds you can use to turn that head on its 360-degree axis. A slow, steady head turn might create a frightened character or a sinister one, whereas a frantic head shake can spell out an emphatic *no* or a moment of disbelief, and a random confusion of left and right turns could imply dizziness from a knock to the head. Use head movements together with the body to give a fuller, more realistic impression—a slow head turn to the front accompanied by a drooping of the upper body is a hopeless minifigure who's given up, while a firm and decisive look away combined with a sharply raised arm suggests a swift "No, thank you!"

The way a prop is held or angled in a minifigure's hand can communicate intention and add variety to your film.
© Paul Hollingsworth

HOW TO ANIMATE

109

Use your own head to act out physical ways to convey thoughts and emotions as a starting point for knowing what do to with your minifigure's head, and then try to convey the following emotions incorporating animation of the head in some way: surprise/shock, sadness, and mischief. Take note of the best results to use in future animations.

Minifigure arms and hands

Minifigures might not have elbows, but what they lack in the synovial hinge joint department, they more than make up for when it comes to their unique claw like mitts. Their hands are angled slightly from their arms, which means that when you position them with the straight side up they'll hold an object away from their body, and when you rotate the hand so the curved side is up, they'll lean the object in slightly toward themselves. Switching between these two options mid-move and rotating the hands in general can create some interesting animation effects.

- If you want your minifigure to perform a hammer blow, position the weapon in the hand with the curved side of the hand facing upward, then when the hammer hits its target, switch the hand upside down so the straight side is facing upward, without changing the orientation of the hammer. It will appear to shift forward, as if the minifigure has swung down with its wrist, adding the appearance of force to the blow.
- Different combinations of twisting and swapping hand positions, not just gradually but suddenly too, from one frame to the next, can create some fun effects, especially if you're trying to create combat scenes.
- Raising a minifigure's arms in the air with the hands curved side up denotes a shrugging of the shoulders or "Why me?" gesture, while doing exactly the same with the hands straight side up can look threatening or angry, perfect for a fist-waving motion.
- To simulate typing, writing, or piano playing, try shooting random and rapid combinations of hand positions.
- Although minifigures are sold with their arms attached, it is possible to remove the arms and switch them around for an unusual-looking backward arm movement—this could be useful for just a few frames in a kung fu fight, a character searching in its pockets, or for a swimming scene.

The power of Blu-Tack

If you're not familiar with Blu-Tack, no doubt there's an equivalent adhesive putty substance you can get hold of where you live, but many professional animators recommend Bostik's Blu-Tack over other products and believe it's perhaps the second greatest off-the-shelf animation tool after LEGO. Why use Blu-Tack?

TOP TIP—HARD TO HANDLE

"Animating a small character in a fiddly and crowded set can be difficult enough and it doesn't come much more fiddly than manipulating minifigure hands," says Tony Mines. "To make small hand movements without accidentally shifting their whole position, use a LEGO spear, pole, or similar tool as a lever to make the movement. Slide it into the minifigure's hand, make the move, and then slide it out again."

- It has great adhesive properties, sticking really well to things, but is equally easy to remove when you're done, which is great for LEGO lovers who don't want to damage their collection.
- It can clean itself up—using a second larger lump to remove a small lump won't disturb the rest of your set, unlike the process required to remove other adhesives.
- It retains its shape and is surprisingly sturdy, meaning you can use it to create a variety of cushioning and support shapes to help your minifigures to perform movements gravity won't allow.
- If you're only going to see it in a few frames, it's possible to animate using the putty without removing it from visible shots—a fast and efficient way to make objects appear to fly.
- Blu-Tack does eventually soften under warm lights, but its melting point is much higher than similar tacks on the market.

Try using Blu-Tack or another similar putty to create a simple effect. A good one to start with is to animate your minifigure leaning or falling backward on its heels or one foot. Use the putty sparingly and for a couple of frames at the most to maximize the effect without giving away the secret. See page 106 for Zach Macias's example in his film *Stranger than Fishin'.*

Director's Chair
Jordon Johnson

I f in-camera effects like flying kicks and lightsaber battles are your thing, then Jordan Johnson's *LEGO: The Force Unleashed* is right up your alley. Read about his experience making the film below and turn to page 114 for more gravity-defying tricks.

What makes a great brick-film?

I think the best advice is before you even start making a brick-film, make sure that you spend enough time to create a story that you really love and are passionate about. The more passionate you are about bringing your story to life, the more dedicated you will be to making it as good as possible. I think that would lead to a successful brick-film.

What do you love about the medium of stop-motion?

I love stop-motion because it's so raw and real. There's something special about watching a stop-motion animation knowing that an animator had to painstakingly move objects in the frame in order to create life. I also specifically love brick-filming because it is so accessible. Most of the things you need you probably already have lying around the house.

How did the Star Wars–centric LEGO: The Force Unleashed come about?

I started an animation challenge on bricksinmotion.com to create a lightsaber duel. So with some healthy competition fueling my fire, I was ready to get going. The funny thing about *The Force Unleashed* is that there really was no plan. I never wrote a script, never storyboarded anything, and the set that I used is very basic. I definitely don't recommend this lack of planning but that's what I did at the time. The only planning that I did is that I wanted to be able to recreate specific fight animations from *The Force Unleashed* video game, and so I watched footage from the game frame by frame in order to figure out how to animate it.

Did this lack of planning cause any problems?

The filming process was fairly straightforward. I usually had a goal for how much animation I wanted to get done in a night and then set to work. Most of the challenges I faced while filming did come about because of my lack of planning. I had to spend a lot of time during production figuring out how the shots that I was animating were going to fit together to make a cohesive scene. Another challenge was the animation. Many of the shots have characters flying through the air, combined with camera movements. I had done these effects before, but

© Jordan Johnson

the difficulty was increased quite a bit with this video.

The fight scene is very elaborate and looks like it took a lot of work–was there anything you couldn't achieve or anything new that you discovered?

One thing that I wasn't able to achieve as much as I wanted is the scale of the fight. I would've liked to have included many more stormtroopers to make the video have a more epic feel. One new idea came when I was trying to film a shot where the camera followed Starkiller from behind as he runs. It was a challenge to figure out how to do this and I ended up doing the shot handheld, picking up and moving the camera for every frame. I wasn't sure how this would work but it turned out surprisingly well.

I imagine quite a lot of time was spent in postproduction. How did you find that?

The biggest part of the postproduction process was adding the lightsaber glow. I ended up creating the glow in Photoshop and then having to place them onto all the individual frames. It was a time-consuming process! I edited the film with Final Cut Express and I was able to find all of the blaster and lightsaber sounds on the Internet from various websites. One of the major decisions that I made was to not include any music in the video. I thought that the fight was more intense with an absence of music so I decided to go without.

How do you feel about the film watching it now?

I think I'm proud of how dynamic the animation turned out to be. It's difficult to create a fight scene with LEGO that doesn't feel robotic, but I was pretty happy with how fluid and smooth it turned out. The reaction was more than I ever expected. When I released the video it quickly became the most popular animation I had ever made and it now has over seven million views on YouTube.

LEGO: The Force Unleashed was shot on a Panasonic PV-GS320. Jordan used iStop-Motion to capture the frames and Final Cut Express and Photoshop in postproduction. To see more of his films go to www.youtube.com/user/xxxfancypantsxxx.

LEGO: The Force Unleashed features a lot of masking work to create the characters' elaborate fight scene.
© Jordan Johnson

DEFYING GRAVITY

You've probably enjoyed a whole host of LEGO animations that seem to defy the laws of physics: fight scenes where LEGO bandits leap across crevasses, LEGO skateboarders showing off their tricks, or even a simple LEGO ball bouncing down the stairs. But how does LEGO fly through the air with the greatest of ease? A little bit of animating trickery, that's how!

The question isn't so much, how do you make LEGO fly, but how do you support airborne objects so they appear to be flying? To achieve this there are a number of options.

Visible supports: multiple techniques

The easiest way to achieve this effect is to leave the support visible, but only for a frame or two so that the audience doesn't really see it. Like any magician knows, the art of distraction is a great way to do this—have a movement elsewhere in the frame that viewers are drawn to and they won't even notice the

This minifigure in Jonathan Vaughan's *Parkour Battle* is showing off his free-running moves with a little help from animation trickery.
© Jonathan Vaughan

support. Or position the support so it's only slightly visible.

Support from behind

Depending on the movement you're trying to create, your object or character can be supported on the end of a pole sticking out of a wall that faces the camera.

If the object is large enough and the camera angle straight on, it will block out the pole altogether.

Invisible plastic sheet

Another clever in-camera method is to film the entire sequence with a sheet of perfectly clear plastic positioned in the middle of the scene from

A good way to practice using supports to defy gravity is by animating a minifigure throwing an object. Here are the key steps:

1. Build up to the throw with a counteraction, such as the thrower leaning backward or readying his or her arm. This way the viewer is prepared for what's to come—they're expecting the ball to be thrown, so to an extent they'll see what they want to see.

2. As the object exits the minifigure's hand, support it forward on a length of Blu-Tack, a LEGO pole, or a small piece of wire.

3. In the next frame, change your support approach so the visible Blu-Tack or wire you used first disappears so quickly the viewer won't spot it. Support the ball from below on another wire, or dangle it from a thread. By changing the supports frequently enough for the length of the throw shot, the one constant—the ball—will be the thing the eye sees, rather than the way it is being supported.

the outset. Be sure to tilt it correctly away from the camera so you achieve an angle where the plastic catches no reflections from your lighting setup and is completely invisible to the camera. Then, to make your objects fly, you can move them along the plastic stuck to a lump of Blu-Tack. Don't forget to clean any Blu-Tack smudges or residue from the plastic after each move.

Postproduction

For filming some sequences, especially where multiple objects are moving through the air, you might prefer to use lots of Blu-Tack, wires, or basic LEGO bricks to build supports for your characters. You can then digitally remove the supports in postproduction. This method might be more time consuming, but will allow you to attach your minifigures to sturdy LEGO towers that you can increase or decrease at incremental rates to create the illusion.

Programs like After Effects and Photoshop offer various ways to cover or erase a support frame by frame or cover it with an animated mask. Whichever method you go for it's likely you're going to need to capture a "plate"—a clean frame of the scene with no moving objects or characters in it (i.e., the background) that will be revealed under the parts of the top image that you erase.

HOW TO ANIMATE

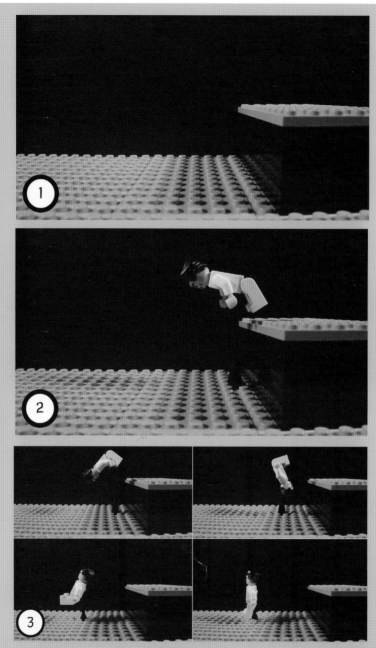

© Daniel Utecht

To defy gravity using postproduction follow these simple steps:

1. Before you start animating, and before you have inserted your moving elements into the shot, capture a frame for your plate.

2. Set up your shot with your character or object being supported in the air with LEGO pieces, or another support of your choice.

3. Capture the image, and repeat until you have captured the whole sequence.
4. Remove the moving elements and capture another shot of the background. This is in case something accidentally moved during filming.
5. Open the plate and one of your "flying" frames in your photo editing software.
6. Layer the flying frame image on top of the plate layer.
7. Use the software's eraser tools to remove the support from the picture. The background image should show through underneath.
8. Don't forget about reflections and shadows. Keep any shadows or reflections of the character and erase any of the support(s).

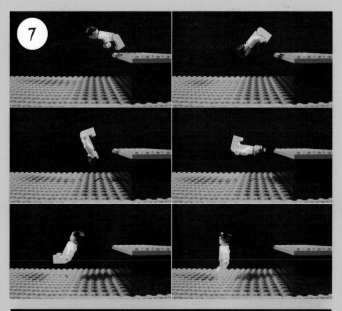

© Daniel Utecht

TOP TIP

If you don't have expensive photo editing software, you can achieve this technique with a lot of free downloads. One free alternative is GIMP (www.getgimp.com).

Sometimes a straightforward idea can really make an impact and leave audiences wanting more. While he has produced a number of longer-form brick-films, *Bovonic Tonic* by David Boddy is one great example of what you can achieve by keeping things simple—part of the short was selected from competition entries to be featured in *The LEGO Movie*.

The transformed cow from *Bovonic Tonic*.
© David Boddy

How were you inspired to start making LEGO stop-motion films?

My initial interest in animation was mostly computer based. In my professional career my duties shifted from computer programming to computer-based modeling and animation. As a result, for recreation I lost interest in 3D computer graphics and animation. That was when I discovered brick-films and decided to make one myself.

There was a big competition running at the time to celebrate the thirtieth anniversary of the LEGO minifigure. I used my video camera to make my first brick-film, *Train to Catch*. I completely underestimated the amount of work

required and ended up having to scrap much of the script. But I was hooked and was destined to make more.

Bovonic Tonic **was another competition entry, correct?**

Yes, I like producing content for competitions as it forces me to work with additional constraints. Having a blank canvas can be daunting with too many possibilities. LEGO also forces me to work within a framework of what can be constructed, which is a challenge I enjoy. The brief was a relatively short film with a hero

that reconstructs his environment to build something to tackle the evil-doer in the movie in a comical way. It also had to use one of the classic LEGO themes. I dreamt up the idea of the mega cow and the only thought I had for its creation was to use a wizard with magic powers.

Other than the mega cow, how did you inject comedy into the film?

The first gag is the introduction of the wizard. The initial shot is quite tight so as not to show his steed. The riding animation is smooth and he looks super cool riding along.

© David Boddy

DIRECTOR'S CHAIR

When the shot changes you see his mount is actually a cow. It's hard to look cool riding a cow, and the animation is exaggerated with his wobbly movement.

How did you create the impressive opening shots with the moving cow and vast landscape?

The landscape used in the background was shot on a different stage. I needed a large area to capture the sideways motion while the wizard is riding along. My lack of bricks forced me to construct a micro scale castle for the background. This had the added benefit of forcing the perspective and making the depth of the shot more epic.

The wizard riding of the cow needed to be clean and smooth. I built a rig that they sat on. A gear was attached to a wheel, which when turned would make the cow slowly rock back and forth. I had a green screen in the background, which could later be keyed out.

The background was shot in real time with a video camera. I made a trolley out of LEGO that the camera sat on, which rolled smoothly past the trees. The slowing down or ease-out of the motion was recorded during that time. I tested this footage underneath the images being recorded in the animation studio to ensure they looked right when married together. The final composition didn't happen until much later in postproduction.

Was there anything you included that wasn't in your original plan for the film?

Often when recording a scene you are there for a long time and other ideas pop up. Ideas also come from just seeing the set and characters within the lens. This has happened many times during every film I've made. The decision to change the transformation animation of cow to mega cow from a puff of smoke to an explosion of the brick potion was one of these last-minute ideas. The contrast of the yellow bricks on everything in the scene was dramatic and I'm much happier with the end result.

In these frames from the transformation sequence, the screen is flooded with yellow bricks.
© David Boddy

What has been the online reaction to the film?

As it was a competition entry I haven't really promoted it a great deal. I have enough subscribers these days to consider them a fan base. I try to make a couple of films a year that are family friendly, mostly for my subscribers. I didn't win the LEGO movie competition with this entry but Warner Bros. liked it enough to award me a gift certificate for their store. I not only made a film I was very happy with and enjoyed making but received a Superman T-shirt, the One Ring, and a Hobbit hoodie. Mission accomplished!

***Bovonic Tonic* was shot using a Logitech Pro 9000 web camera and a Sony HD video camera. It was edited using Adobe Premiere and Photoshop. David also used The Helium Frog Animator. Check out his films and loads of behind the scenes extras on: www.youtube.com/user/pe668.**

MULTIPLE PASS SEQUENCES

This refers to shooting multiple elements of the same scene separately, rather than all at once. The main reason you might do this is because the complexity of a shot demands this approach. If you have multiple characters moving around at once, you might prefer to animate them one or two at a time, and add in different visual effects to each sequence, or you might use this method if there are certain background props or characters that you want to be moving on a loop, unlike your foreground characters. Shooting a sequence more than once can be the most efficient way to achieve this.

Multiple pass sequences are achieved using layers in your editing or visual effects software. Software used by professionals including After Effects, Premiere, Final Cut, and others can be used to combine different takes or "passes" of the same shot. Essentially, you require a program that can treat your sequence file as a layer and overlay it with other sequences. The software should then allow you to mask off unwanted areas of the image using a number of tools—these range from simple geometric shapes to pencil/knife tools, which can accurately cut out the specific shape you want

to mask. You will be able to animate your masks frame by frame or use "key frames" so that they change over time, following the shape of your animations. Other tools in your software should allow you to soften the edges of these masks, to avoid harsh visible lines when the sequences are layered.

Here are just some instances where this technique will come in handy:

- To combine separate animation elements, as described previously.
- To mask out stands and supports for flying and gravity-defying actions, as explained earlier in the chapter.
- To remove mistake areas, such as trails of Blu-Tack or paper reflectors that have fallen into your shot.
- To add objects to the scene—for example, putting back a wall or ceiling that you wanted to remove to have better animation access.
- To combine live video with your animation sequences—for example, animating minifigures moving in the foreground, while live action of your cat walking past goes on in the

HOW TO ANIMATE

background. Don't forget, if you're combining with video then make sure the frame rates of both sequences match up and that your exposures and settings are the same for your video and photography.

- See the next section for using a rotoscope layer to help you line up different passes and avoid myriad problems.

Multiple pass sequence reminders

- Don't forget to capture a "background plate," as described earlier in the "defying gravity" section. This should contain no movable objects or characters. This plate will be used to fill any empty space left between your various masked layers. Make sure you take one shot before and one after you animate. This will

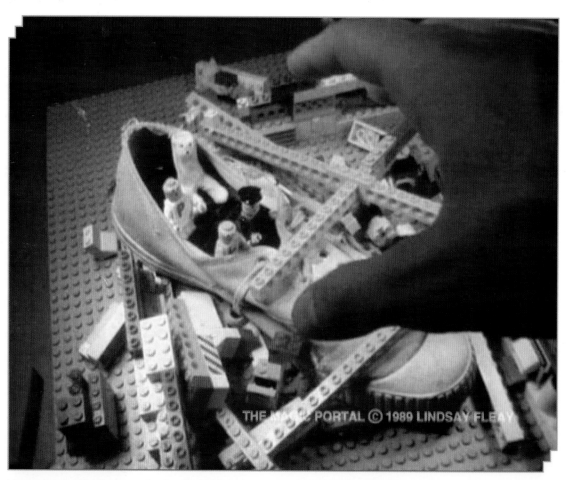

Live action is blended seamlessly with LEGO in Lindsay Fleay's *The Magic Portal*.
© Lindsay Fleay

give you options to play with in case anything moves or the lights change.

- Take the time to map out the space where the actions will take place to avoid any problematic overlaps from the various sequences. For example, do you know how far to the right your character is going to run and how high to the left the other character is going to jump? It's this kind of precision and organization that will make the process a lot smoother.

- Just because you're shooting a sequence more than once, don't let all your animating rules go out the window. Remember to think about the effect your characters and objects are having on the space around them, not just the physical space they are taking up. If you don't take the time to look at the background, the light on your characters, the shadows they're creating, and so on, then you might end up with layers of varying colors, shadows slashed in half, and a rather amateur-looking final cut.

ROTOSCOPE ANIMATION

In 2D animation, rotoscoping is tracing over live video, frame by frame, to create a realistic or hyperrealistic drawn animation. In stop-motion, rotoscoping can be used to copy in the same way, either using 2D images or video footage to instruct or guide the animator. This footage, laid over your animation workspace, can be used for timing—either timing your animation to previously shot sequences, or to other materials. If you're combining multiple passes of a single shot, then uploading your previous pass or passes as rotoscoped layers will help you to accurately time the new pass.

Some animators will upload a live-action video and recreate it frame by frame in their new medium, in this case LEGO. How about choosing your favorite music video and then using it as a rotoscoped layer to perfectly time a shot-by-shot LEGO version?

While this is a fast and efficient way to animate a sequence, it's not recommended that you rely too heavily on using rotoscope layers in this way. Not only does animation timing differ from live-action timing, giving it that otherworldly quality, one of the important things to develop as an animator is your own style of creating characters through their movement. Minifigures are not the same as human subjects, and are never going to move in the same way. This should be used to your advantage, exploiting the different ways minifigures can move for dramatic and comedic effect, rather than trying to accurately replicate human movements. If you open up your rotoscope layer next to your animation window, you can use it as a guide, creating similar movements with your minifigures and LEGO models, using your own unique style to exaggerate and bring character to the sequence.

You might also use a rotoscope layer to animate on top of your stop-motion sequence with special effects. These might be laser beams, which you've drawn yourself, or magical effects that you've created using VFX software. Using programs like After Effects, you can use paint tools and other effects to draw over your animated sequence, enhancing the final film.

Film a short sequence using real people or find a short clip online, from a music video or a film that you like. Choose something fairly simple with some obvious movement or action. Import and load up this video into your stop-motion animation software and, using the rotoscope function, practice either copying or exaggerating real movements, frame-by-frame for an interesting effect.

Making the Most of Your Set

You might have spent weeks in production prepping, building, and arranging the various elements of your studio, from your storyboard and lighting to the LEGO sets you've created, so it's important to not rush the animation part of production. It might seem frustrating at first, as capturing just a few seconds for your film will take time, but after all that effort now is not the time to lose your enthusiasm. When you've shot everything you think you need for a particular setup, check back through your sequence to see if there's anything that could be improved, anything you accidentally skipped or forgot to animate, and any other way you might want to do something to give you options at the editing stage. Unless you have the luxury of crates full of LEGO, chances are you will be demolishing this set to build another one, so don't tear it down until you're confident you don't need it anymore. David Boddy is an advocate of this approach. "Sometimes I'll record scenes over and over to get them right," he says. "So much time is invested with the sets and props, lighting, scene composition so I want to do it all justice before pulling the scene down. I may get everything right on the first attempt but it's rare. The first run through is often to get practice with all the moving parts of a scene and how to track what is occurring."

I n 2002, The White Stripes were looking for someone to make the music video for their hit song "I Fell in Love with a Girl." Michel Gondry, director of *Eternal Sunshine of the Spotless Mind*, *The Science of Sleep*, and *The Green Hornet*, got the job by a fortuitous mistake. And the rest is LEGO block and roll history.

Were you presented with the idea of a LEGO stop-motion music video by The White Stripes, or did you come up with it? What inspired you to go down this route?

I had just bought the LEGO Studios camera for my son. We started to experiment together. I'd done some abstract LEGO animation with it and I thought that would fit the song, because the song is very punk. I thought the simplicity of the LEGO and the simplicity of the colors matched it quite well. When I met Jack and Meg [of The White Stripes], I had built Jack's head with LEGO blocks to show them. They were immediately into it.

They had seen a Lenny Kravitz video for the song "Are You Gonna Go My Way," which is an amazing video. And they wanted to work with whoever directed this video and mistakenly they thought it was me. And so they met me on the basis of that. But once they saw the concept of the LEGO blocks, they changed their minds and said, "OK, we'll do it with Michel."

How much of the film was storyboarded in advance, and how much was a product of playing with the bricks?

We shot a very classical video, with very small video cameras, just

Jack White's 3D LEGO head, which Michel Gondry used to convince the band to shoot a LEGO music video.

having them play on their instruments. I put a lot of makeup on their eyes—actually, Jack looked a bit like the guy from The Cure, Robert Smith. And I asked them to swim in the swimming pool, and they were running in the street. We were in London, so I shot some traffic passing by; some red buses because it would be easy to reproduce with LEGO. After that we edited the footage into a video. Then my father made a program to print out all the images at the definition of LEGO blocks with the shape of the LEGO blocks like big pixels. We had one printed frame per image and I hired a team of ten people to animate that. So they would construct a LEGO wall, which we shot with the 16mm Bolex camera, and then we would demolish it and rebuild another one and so on.

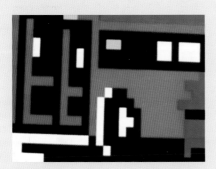

You can just make out the red London LEGO bus during its brief appearance in the short music video.

Why did you decide to stick with the traditional LEGO color palette and avoid the more recent colors?

When I was a kid in the sixties there were only black, white, yellow, red, and blue. Never green, never brown, never orange. It was a good idea for The White Stripes

because they had this concept that they would use red and blue and white. First they wanted me to use only those three colors, but I said it [was] important to use the five colors of the brand, the initial colors, so they went along with it.

How long did you spend shooting the video and how big was the team?

Overall it was one month, but I think in animation it was two or three weeks. There were ten or twelve animators and they were pretty efficient.

Were there any ideas deemed too ambitious for the time frame or did you get to include everything you wanted?

I included everything because basically the limitation was set at the beginning—we would work with these LEGO blocks at this scale. And there are just two shots where we doubled the definition, by building the surface of the wall four times larger and you can really tell that they're much more defined.

Did you enjoy using LEGO as a medium? How did you find the process of shooting?

It was really exciting. I liked this idea that you're very limited in the definition and you have to manage to get the image across although it's very crude. I've played with LEGO throughout my youth since I was a kid and I've always loved the system.

Was the LEGO Group involved at all?

What was funny was at the time LEGO was not at all interested in this project, and they were somewhat against it because they thought the image of The White Stripes was not fitting the image of LEGO. They didn't provide any LEGO blocks and later on when they saw the video they wanted to make a deal with The White Stripes so they could use their popularity for their brand, but The White Stripes said, "No, no, it's too late now."

At what point did you realize this was going to be a really amazing use of the medium? Was it hard to see how it was all going to come together until the end?

I'd shot some tests, but because the video was very simple and you couldn't recognize the faces, I was a bit worried. Sometimes when I do things in the beginning, I'm not sure if there's a special quality, but as time passed by it became more noticeable, and I felt better and better about it. It was more than ten years ago, but I feel that it's ageless in a way. The combination of shooting on 16mm and doing something as sophisticated as this is a good combination.

A lot of videos have been made with LEGO since and sometimes people think some are more complex and say comments like, "That should teach [Michel Gondry] a lesson," but I did it first. Maybe I was not the first person to animate LEGO, but I think I was the first one to do it to this scale. I tried to make something really dynamic. We made a very magical video because we had no narration, no style really to think of, so it was complete freedom just to do something with a lot of energy.

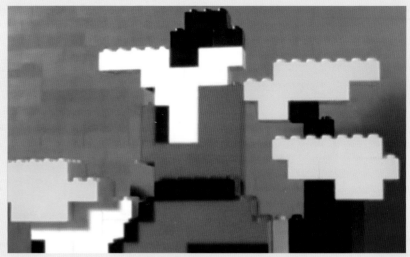

Meg White from The White Stripes made from LEGO bricks.

You've directed so many music videos over the years, and obviously much larger feature-film projects. Does this experience stand out for you in any way?

We had to work on it somewhat blindly, because when we shot the animation we didn't shoot it digitally so we had to finish many shots before we got the film back. This wait, because it had to go to the lab and then be transferred back to DVD before we could watch it, this sort of patience, the surprise you get . . . Sometimes when I shoot my movies I think, OK, maybe I should not look at the shot right away. Often I don't want to look in between the shot because it slows down the process and I want to

preserve the surprise, and I think this habit comes from doing this video.

What would be your advice to other filmmakers looking to try out stop-motion using LEGO bricks?

When you do stop-motion animation, if you are patient enough to do small displacements in each frame, then it's going to accelerate more nicely, smoothly. Sometimes when people start they're too impatient so they make big gaps between the images and then it's too jumpy. You don't have to be a professional animator, but if you take the patience to move things, either drawings or shapes, if you move little bit by little bit, then it becomes really smooth and magical.

So patience is the key?

I'm not really patient in general, but what's good with animation is you really get to know the value of a second, even more a minute—you know you have to do twenty-four frames to achieve one second so you have a sense of the time you're spending. And when you watch the result you know that each second means a lot of work. I think creative people need reward, even if it's just for ourselves. Doing animation and watching the completed shot, it's a great reward—it gives you the energy to do the next one.

To find out what director Michel Gondry is up to these days head to his website www.michelgondry.com.

OTHER TYPES OF LEGO ANIMATION

The idea of a LEGO figure wasn't introduced until the 1970s. Prior to the 1974 release of the Family Set, children had to make do with building structures, vehicles, and their own little people built from the more limited array of LEGO bricks. The minifigure as we know it today was first available as a policeman in 1978 and, other than the introduction of varied facial expressions and skin tones, the fundamentals of the figure haven't changed since. Most people come to LEGO stop-motion wanting to film stories that involve mini-figures, and this method is a great introduction to stop-motion, but once your confidence increases, you might want to think about trying to use your LEGO collection in other ways. Here are just some ideas to get you started.

Use non-minifigure LEGO characters from Bionicle or Hero Factory, or build your own using LEGO parts. This is a behind-the-scenes shot from Digital Wizards' *LEGO Lord of the Rings: Two Towers in Two Minutes.*
© Paul Hollingsworth

Armature Animation/Articulated Figures

If you're a fan of LEGO then you know that minifigures aren't the only characters those Danish wizards produce. Over the years LEGO has been responsible for a whole range of articulated figures from Technic, DUPLO, and LEGO Friends—slightly larger figures to Ninjago's mech, Hero Factory, Bionicle, and Mixels. The range of larger figures that you can bring to your stop-motion films is vast.

By opting to animate with larger figures, you're stepping further into the realms of traditional claymation and the use of armatures—frameworks, often made from stainless steel, onto which a character is molded. These skeletons are not that different from a Bionicle figure, which has impressive pose-ability, so it's a good idea to watch films such as the *Wallace & Gromit* features and *ParaNorman*, which use armature models, to get some inspiration for your videos.

With the added articulation that these larger figures have, you'll be able to create more nuanced, realistic movements and replicate human physicality more easily. There is a true art to animation with this level of physical detail, and a whole other book could be filled on the techniques professional animators use, but it's safe to say that harnessing all the universal rules we've already covered for minifigure animation applies to larger models too.

To read up more about the observation of human (and animal) motion captured through photography, visit Kingston University and the Kingston Museum's collaborative research site on the work of photographer Eadweard Muybridge (www.eadweardmuybridge.co.uk).

Replacement Animation

While most stop-motion animations feature armature models, there are some elements, or in some cases entire films, where replacement animation is used instead. This is where rather than molding or adjusting a singular figure to achieve the required movement or expression, the model is swapped out for each frame and replaced with another that is incrementally or extremely different. With LEGO this can be used when you want the object to appear to change size and shape noticeably—a model of a small green shoot can be switched out for a slightly larger plant, and then a larger one, until it becomes a tree. Other uses include: switching between sloped pieces with varying inclines or widths to change the shape of the slope, switching identical pieces of different colors for a flashing, magical result—think fairy wands or portals to other dimensions, creating water, fire, and laser effects, as well as replacing minifigure heads with ones that have different expressions (or twisting around the ones with reverse expressions). Replacement animation can be sudden and extreme or gradual and subtle—it's up to you and your film how you choose to use it.

For his film *Jane's Brain,* Chris Salt used replacement animation to create the effect of a car tearing up the grass as it sped away. "There were little trenches built into the ground where the tyre tracks would appear," he says. "For the 'before' areas, the trenches were filled in with green plates and for the 'after' areas, brown plates. It's the sort of fun trick you can only really do with stop-motion." He also added in tyre smoke by turning gray and brown 1 × 1 round plates into little smoke puffs that appeared behind the car as it moved forward.

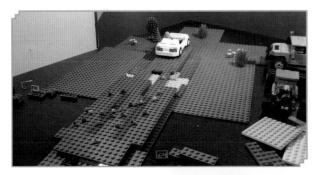

Chris Salt's use of replacement animation to create the illusion of the ground being churned up in *Jane's Brain*. He used Blu-Tack to position bits of flying earth as the car sped away.
© Chris Salt

Use replacement animation to create the illusion of a flashing cop car light or to make your minifigure switch moods in an instant by replacing his head.

Small replacement animation moments can be simple to achieve an effect in your film, such as here with the car's flashing lights.
© Paul Hollingsworth

MOVING THE CAMERA

As you become a more confident animator, it will probably dawn on you that for a filmmaker you don't touch the camera at all. Panning or tracking shots, and other camera movements, are a great way to add visual interest to your films. Physically moving the camera might seem like the most obvious way to create those movements, but doing this frame by frame is actually quite a cumbersome and frustrating process, especially for beginners. Even with a very good, expensive, "fluid head" to your tripod that allows for flexibility movements, the time you have to spend to adjust the camera *and* animate your LEGO characters could be more work than you'd like. Without such a tripod it's very difficult to move your camera in a subtle and fluid way and you'll more than likely end up with big jerky movements that ruin the look of your film. More annoyingly, if you make a mistake or want to go back to reshoot something from a previous position, it's nearly impossible to realign the camera.

To avoid these frustrations, it makes more sense to keep the camera still and make everything else move, especially where LEGO is concerned. LEGO's systematic design enables you to create reliable, moveable setups. By counting studs you can move your sets by measureable increments, moving things in front of the camera accurately. You can push baseplates forward and back, relying on the straight, sturdy holding construction to return things to precisely the same place when you're done or you can build sets that can be slid between walls.

For those more technically minded filmmakers, LEGO Technic provides ever more solutions to your mechanical problems—how about building a cog-controlled rig to move your set? Combinations of moving backgrounds and firmly located objects can also be used to create the illusion of a camera movement. When working camera moves into your film, don't be afraid to experiment or change the camera framing to make your life easier. For example, sometimes you might not need to move the whole set—if you wanted to film a car driving past moving scenery, a shot through a side window would only require some trees on a baseplate to be moving for it to appear that the whole car is travelling by. And don't forget to ease in and out for a smooth, realistic effect.

There are some other ways you can create camera moves—most notably in postproduction. Turn to page 165 to find out more.

Christian Colglazier used this tripod/camera setup for his film *CON*. "In the past I used software to create the illusion of camera motion," he says. "For this I used a new tripod that had a fluid head which allows for alteration in how fast the tripod moves and very precise movements."
© Christian Colglazier

Three frames from one of Christian's camera panning shots.
© Christian Colglazier

FILMMAKING AND STORYTELLING

6

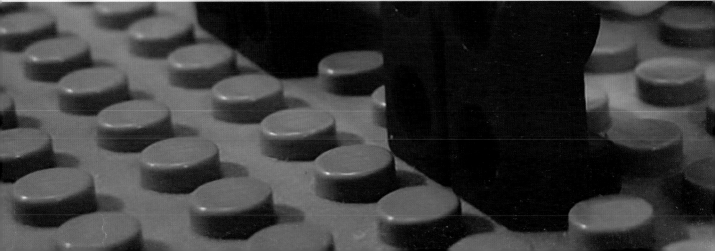

Now that you have started to develop some of the basic animating skills required to shoot your first brick-film, you've probably started to think about the kind of films you want to make and how to make them. You might be asking questions such as: How do I know if my idea is any good? How do I tell a story using cuts and camera angles? How do I know what order to shoot my scenes in? This chapter focuses on how to be a good filmmaker, rather than how to make a good film—the reason being, that by adhering to some rudimentary filmmaking techniques, your film is more likely to tell the story you want to tell.

IDEAS AND INSPIRATION

When you're starting out with stop-motion, there's no need to make films that appeal to anyone but you. You're making them for your own enjoyment, so the content and the way you present it is subject to your tastes. However, after you've built up your confidence, it's a fair assumption that you're going to want to share your work with others, either in person or via websites like YouTube. You might want to share your films purely to receive advice and an audience reaction, to help you improve your skills, or to showcase a particular technique you've been practicing. But you're also probably going to want to entertain. This is important, because the more you learn how to entertain people the better reactions you'll get. Learning how to engage, surprise, and even manipulate your audience (in a nice way, of course!) is really the key to good filmmaking. After all, you don't want to bore people with your films.

There are no hard and fast rules that say your brick-film has to tell a story, or have a happy ending, or even make any sense, but if you can keep in your head at all times that somebody will have to watch your film, it should help you to create something that *gives* to the audience, rather than merely taking up their time. Of course every film has to start somewhere, and getting a great idea that you want to commit to can be almost as hard as animating it (almost!) Taking inspiration from others is a good way to get started—although outright copying is frowned on. If there's something someone else has done—be it as a brick-film, in the movies, on TV, or some element of pop culture that appeals to you—think about how you can develop it to work in the LEGO environment, and what you can do differently to make it your own. Here are how some of the animators featured in this book come up with their ideas.

Christian Colglazier

"Most of my ideas and inspiration come from what I read and watch. I am an avid science fiction reader and I find that leads me to ideas for films. I also find that watching movies helps to inspire my visual looks. I look for shot angles I like in movies and techniques that I could use in future films. I also pull from things I learn from going about my normal life."

David Boddy

"Cartoons are a great source of inspiration, but the quality of them varies greatly. The masterful works of Disney and Warner Bros. during the thirties and forties were replaced with cheap production in cartoons like *Scooby-Doo*. I love the work of Buster Keaton and Chaplin for the slapstick visuals and comedic timing. Today I enjoy *Robot Chicken* and although the jokes aren't always super funny, the stop-motion animation is inspiring."

Jonathan Vaughan

"All my best film ideas came about accidentally, without me trying to have an idea. I find that, for me, this is the best way to approach the creative process. It's impossible to force creativity. You have to create a space where it comes about naturally. Once I have a concept in place, everything else comes easily if I just dedicate time to thinking about it. I think it is also important to have an open mind, and not classify anything as 'right' or 'wrong' in the initial brainstorming stage. At times I've found my inner critic severely limiting my creative abilities because I'm being too picky about ideas."

Zach Macias

"Inspiration is a funny thing for me; it eludes me when I need it and strikes me when I least expect it. Since I've started brick-filming, I've taken a keen interest in film and cinema, and have watched a lot of movies over the last several years. If it hasn't helped influence how I create my ideas, at the very least, it has influenced the way I look at storytelling. I study techniques that different directors use to tell their stories, and in turn, that has influenced the way that I choose to visualize my ideas. I feel it helps my understanding of what works, what doesn't, and that even can help to shape an initial concept into a full, scriptable story.

"Sometimes, if you think you have a good idea, or even a good scene or shot, you've just got to go for it and trust your vision, because you'll never know if it was a good idea until you try it out. And sometimes, that's all it really comes down to—trying things out and seeing what works and what doesn't, and building off of that."

As Zach Macias says, it's easy to be put off by the thought of an idea. Perhaps you have visions of a Roman amphitheater filled with characters or you want to shoot a scene in outer space, but the thought of how you will create the world in your small studio space is putting you off. Animation is an art based on problem solving. Don't worry about how you're going to make something look real. Just write a script or a story that incorporates everything and anything you want to include and *then* figure out how you're going to achieve it. There might be some ideas that you can solve easily, others which take a bit of trial and error, and others you might abandon due to financial or time constraints, but this is what animation is all about. Don't stop before you've even started.

SCRIPTS, STORYBOARDS, AND SHOT LISTS

Some of the filmmakers in this book don't use scripts, storyboards, and shot lists, but all three can be useful tools in helping to think about your film in terms of its length, narrative flow, and entertainment value as well as planning out what you're going to shoot and the order you're going to shoot it in.

Scripts

It was Alfred Hitchcock who said, "To make a great film you need three things: the script, the script, and the script." Whether your script is one page or one hundred pages, includes dialogue or doesn't, this is your film in its entirety written down for all to see. If your film is dialogue-driven

The characters from Jonathan Vaughan's *Zombie: Genesis* look over their storyboard.
© Jonathan Vaughan

the script will be based around that, and if it's not it will be based more around the written descriptions of each scene and the action that takes place. As your script will probably just be for your eyes only (unless you're using other voice actors), the information you include is entirely up to you, but it might be worth considering including the following:

- Time of day and location of each scene—This will help you to know what lighting setup to use and which set you're going to need.
- Character descriptions—If you are asking other people to voice your characters for you a small description or picture of the minifigure you're using will help them to understand the voice you want for the character.
- Dialogue—By writing out all the dialogue you'll have a better idea of the length of your film. It's also important for establishing if certain jokes or lines work and make sense to the audience.

- Stage directions—If there are any props or actions that are essential to the storytelling (e.g., a character picks up a red bag, which will be stolen in the next scene), then it's worth including them in the scene so you don't forget and have to reshoot later.
- Other notes—During preproduction or even while you're shooting, you might think of a great visual joke or moment you want to include somewhere in the film. Having a script allows you to work this in later on and see how it will fit with the overall shape of the story.

A script can be some handwritten notes on a legal pad or a simple text document, but if you're planning a lengthier production you might want to use some specially designed script-writing software. No need to spend money on this, although Final Draft and Movie Magic Screenwriter are popular pay-for programs, as there are free downloads that will do the job just fine including Celtx and Page 2 Stage.

dam Radwell's hugely popular take on the song "Summer Nights" from the film *Grease* is a good example of using an existing structure or medium as a reference point to practice your stop-motion skills. While he didn't use a rotoscope layer to match the movements precisely, he did study the existing film frame by frame to help him create his storyboards. A great idea if you're stuck for inspiration!

The famous cafeteria scene from *Grease* brick-film style.
© Adam Radwell

Was the *Grease: Summer Nights* video your first foray into stop-motion with LEGO bricks?

It was my first major animation that I completed. I had done a number of small animations prior to this, however they were only for fun and to experiment with different styles and techniques of animation. I made this animation as part of my university dissertation project. The reason that I chose to do the *Grease* song was because I wanted to do a scene from a popular movie that would be instantly recognizable, even when using LEGO.

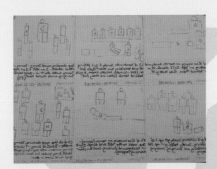

Part of Adam's detailed storyboard from the film.

Why did you decide to use LEGO over other toys or model options?

The main reason that I opted for LEGO was you don't need to worry about them falling over, so you can concentrate on making the rest of the animation perfect. I've done another animation using Action Man and Barbie, which was unbelievably hard; they kept falling over and making them walk, let alone dance, was a struggle. I wouldn't say LEGO is the easy option, but it is a lot easier than most options for stop-motion animation.

Which part of the video was the hardest to produce and why?

If I am honest I don't think there was an "easy" part of the film.

Stop-motion animation is challenging in the fact you have to have a lot of patience to complete it. One slight error and you have to start the whole scene again. It was extremely tricky making Danny stand up and then also jump in one of the scenes. Thankfully the wonders of Blu-Tack assisted me in overcoming this obstacle. As I spread the animating out over various days I would have to make sure everything was the same as the previous day and ensure the continuity was spot on, which is another challenge in itself.

What new stop-motion skills did you learn during the shoot?

Before I completed the actual animation I spent a few months playing about with different techniques and skills to animate the LEGO. Before I started I had next to no knowledge or experience of stop-motion, other than messing about when I was a kid. Everything I did for this animation was learnt over the nine-month period that I spent researching, completing and analysing my dissertation.

© Adam Radwell

How did you feel about the video when it was finished?

Buzzing! The feeling you get seeing the finished product after you have spent hours upon hours creating it is incredible. It is such a rewarding feeling; the buzz is definitely worth the hours, labor, stress, and anger that you put into it. Even now, after a good few years, I still love watching it back and I always have a huge smile on my face knowing that it was my hard work and determination that created the video. The fact it has over two million views on YouTube is another factor that makes me extremely pleased with my efforts; that in itself is a reward.

Are you surprised by the millions of views the video has already received on YouTube?

Very much so. The response I have had on YouTube is incredible. The reason I originally put it on there was to show my mum and dad, but from there it slowly took off and most people seem to like it. Everyone knows the song, and it is one of those songs that you can't help but sing along to. It is light-hearted and different. I might be biased but I think it can only bring a smile to your face when watched.

If you were to produce the film again would you make any changes or do anything differently?

I used a MiniDV camera so it isn't the best quality and isn't widescreen. If I were to remake it, it would have to be in HD and widescreen so I can make it the best quality possible. Another change

that would be important would be the top that I used for Sandy. Unfortunately, part of the top was removed as a result of the green screen that I used, so I would need to look at alternatives as to how I can ensure this wouldn't happen again. Lastly, I would love to have the minifigures' mouths moving as they sing.

In this split-screen image you can see the problem with the green screen effect on Sandy's top.

Do you have any tips or advice for others looking to try stop-motion using LEGO?

I would say be patient and don't give up. It can be incredibly frustrating; however, the end result is well worth the time you put in. The feeling you get when you see the completed video is fantastic! And also make sure you have fun doing it. . . . Just enjoy yourself!

Adam's *Grease* film was shot using a MiniDV camera and the animation was captured using Monkey Jam. You can watch it on his YouTube channel: www.youtube.com/user/ demondoggz.

Storyboards

A storyboard is a visual interpretation of your script that shows how the story will be told. All you'll need for this is a piece of paper divided up into frames. Sketch in the basic movements of the story and write notes underneath to explain your drawings. You don't need to be a fine artist to create a storyboard—remember this is a guide for you and no one else so don't waste time trying to make the drawings accurate. More importantly, show the kind of angles and action you want to capture. For example, will there be a wide shot of a city scape that moves into a close-up? Will there be any aerial shots or extreme close-ups on your characters? When the characters are fighting, how will you shoot it and from what angles? Although

you can figure this stuff out when you're shooting, it's much better to have an overview of the film's visuals.

For some animators this tool is priceless. When Adam Radwell wanted to make a brick-film of a song from *Grease*, he used a storyboard to work out how he was going to create each shot using LEGO. When it came to shooting the film some of the shots were improvised but the storyboard helped him to stay on track. "As you can see from my storyboards, my drawing is not very good," says Adam, "however, to counteract this I include as much written information as possible. I highlighted the main characters using letters, included the length of each shot, the number of frames, shot type, and details of what happened in each shot."

Zach Boivin's storyboard from *The Gold Getaway.*
© Zach Boivin

Shot lists

Making a list of all the shots you need to capture and the order you're going to shoot them in is the most efficient way of keeping your film on track and production moving steadily. If you've planned the film carefully this will save you a huge amount of time, because you'll always know what's coming next. It's also a visual aid that illustrates how much of the film you've completed and how much is left to go. Ticking shots off is rewarding and will help motivate you. The list can be numbered or coded to relate to your storyboard and should be written in the order you want to shoot the film. The order you shoot in will depend on a number of factors, which will be unique to each film you make, but with limited space and a sole animator you're going to want to make the most of each lighting/set configuration to avoid wasting time. See "continuity filming in stop-motion" beginning on page 148 for more about how to order your shot list.

Practice turning ideas into structured production schedules. Come up with a simple three-scene idea for a short brick-film. Write that idea into a script including any dialogue and information about the set/props/characters, etc. Then devise a storyboard, breaking down each scene in order, and think about it visually—what kind of shots are you going to use? How will they relate to each other? When your storyboard's complete write a shot list to determine the most efficient order to shoot all the action.

FILMIC STORYTELLING: THE BASICS

" I often make a film purely to support the animation I want to do or a technique I want to learn," says David Boddy. "This is the polar opposite to good story telling. You are meant to create animation to support the story you are telling and not create a story to support the animation." It's important to keep this in mind when you're planning on how to film a particular scene. What you shoot and the way you shoot it should be bolstering the narrative, communicating something with your audience. That might be a clear back-and-forth conversation between two characters or a frenetic fight scene where the audience is made to feel disoriented. Either way, make sure that the way you shoot the scene tells the story for you.

The 180-degree rule

This is a basic principle applied to filming whereby the camera should never cross the spatial line between two characters. If one character is to the left of the screen facing toward another character who is to the right of the screen, there is an invisible axis between them and a 180-degree arc that the camera can film from. If the camera crosses over that arc then the character that was previously to the left of the camera will now appear on the right. It's unlikely that you will be moving your camera much at all, but remember not to cross over this line as it may disorient the audience.

Shot composition

Knowing what shot works best for each moment of a scene is something you will naturally come to appreciate. While it is possible to shoot an entire scene using just one shot type and positioning, by including a variety in your films they will be more visually engaging and your characters will come to life.

There are five basic types of shots that you can use in any type of filmmaking. These are:

1. **Extreme close-up**—Used when you want to frame a small detail of an object or character. This will make it larger than life-size and is an intimate shot that will probably be used sparingly.

2. **Close-up**—Used when you want to communicate emotions or a deeper understanding for the audience—for example a character's

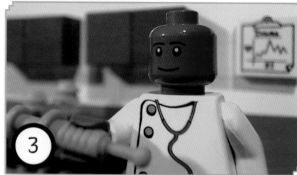

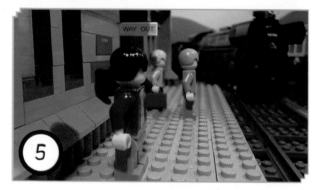

© Chris Salt

head or their hands. This will help to draw the audience's attention to the character over the background.

3. **Mid/Medium shot**—This is a slightly wider shot that shows (in the case of a character) half of his or her body. It's useful for framing individual characters in conversation with one another.

4. **Long shot**—This shot will show the whole character and the situation he or she is in. You might choose to use this framing as an establishing shot for some scenes so the audience can appreciate the environment and the character(s) within it.

5. **Extreme Long/Wide shot**—If you really want to emphasise the environment over the

character(s) then you will need a wide shot. As LEGO minifigures and your sets are likely to be relatively small, it's unlikely you'll need to shoot a lot of wide shots in most films, but if you build a bigger set then this is a great way to let the camera appreciate it.

This low-angle shot is perfect to capture the bad guy in Jonathan Vaughan's *Red Eye*.
© Jonathan Vaughan

By adjusting the angle of any of these shot types you can create atmosphere and tell the story—for example, a low-angled mid-shot looking up at a tall villainous character will help to establish that character's power and dominance over other characters, while a bird's eye view of the action can be used to show a character's point of view if he or she is falling or flying.

Aspect ratio

This refers to the ratio of the frame's horizontal and vertical measurements. Most TV shows use a 4:3 or 16:9 aspect ratio, which is also likely to be the same as the native image from your camera. When you're animating it's a good idea to study the dimensions of your primary subject and adjust the aspect ratio to suit it. Minifigures are short and wide compared to humans, and for this reason they lend themselves to a wider, more dramatic aspect ratio like 2.40:1, which will allow you to fit more into your image horizontally—for instance, including three characters in a shot instead of two. So for minifigure-based films, take your framing inspiration from wide-screen movies. You can easily create wide-screen bars in most editing software or use an overlay you've created in a paint program.

Match cuts

When thinking of how shots will transition between one another, it's useful to think about the way action is shown in a comic book, guiding you around the page. If one of your characters walks off screen to the left, you are leading the audience to expect to see what happens left of the screen. Your next shot could be of the character standing in a doorway about to leave the room or a left-set close-up on his or her face as they leave. You might also use match cuts to take audiences from one scene to another—a shot of a child falling asleep with a shot of them waking up the next day. The audience will understand from the lighting and sound that time has passed and it is now morning.

Cutting on action

This refers to when, in the middle of an action sequence, you cut to a shot from another angle of the action. This creates an impression of continuous motion and because the action is identical from one shot to the next, just from a different viewpoint, the viewer won't notice the cut, but it will serve to make the scene energetic.

Jump cuts and cross cuts

If your intention is to disorient the audience, you can create deliberate discontinuity by using jump cuts and cross cuts. The former is when you cut from one scene to another that is similar but not identical, so a "jump" in the action occurs, and the audience notices. The latter is when you cut back and forth between different unrelated spaces to create confusion. A deliberate cross cut can also make it clear to an audience that the action has changed location.

Continuity filming in stop-motion

When filming live action on a typical set, directors might choose to use multiple cameras to capture the same scene from a variety of angles simultaneously, for example a close-up of two actors' faces as they talk and a wider shot capturing them both in conversation. While shooting with more than one camera is possible with stop-motion, it's not widely used. This is because your set might only be shootable from one angle (as you might only have built two LEGO walls, for example). A slight angle change from where your primary camera is set up will probably reveal hidden supports and lighting mechanisms that you don't want to show anyway. Because of this, all the continuity in stop-motion has to be faked, as on a one-camera TV show. If your characters are having a conversation, for instance, and you want to alternate between two close-up shots, it makes far more sense to shoot all the shots for one character's lines in one go and then move the set to capture all of the other's.

With LEGO it's often easier to rearrange the whole scene rather than move the camera, so once your camera is set up and your lighting is prepped for a particular angle, it makes sense to capture everything you're going to need from that point of view, then reset the lighting and the set for any reverse shots or other angles you want to capture. This is why a shot list is useful as you will be able to group shots by the set they use, and the angle and shot type that they require. It should reduce the amount of time your film takes to shoot.

THE JOKE'S ON YOU

LEGO stop-motion is intrinsically humorous— tiny little plastic men who don't bend in all the usual places, waddling around in their tiny plastic world. What's not to laugh at? However, the harder you work to establish the reality of the world you're creating, the more normal the

These funny shorts from Chris Salt take recognizable characters and put them in outlandish scenarios with great comedic results.
© Chris Salt

minifigures will look to the viewer and the harder you will have to work to make them find your film amusing. Humor can come from the initial idea or setup of a scene, the dialogue, physical character comedy, and even small visual touches such as background characters, scenery, and props. Jonathan Vaughan's films use combinations of these to make funny films that deserve repeated viewing. Here are his top tips for comedy gold.

- To know if a joke works, I go with my gut reaction. If it feels right to me, I use it. But it's essential to have a few trusted friends who will give you honest and detailed feedback on a script.

- The process of evaluating a joke does not stop at the writing stage. When recording the dialog with an actor, I will evaluate again if I think the joke is working or not. Sometimes, I reach the recording stage and something that sounded good on paper isn't funny when the actor says it. Often this can be corrected by giving the actor a direction to change their performance, but sometimes it can't be fixed and the joke needs to be cut.

- The visual component of the animation can also affect a joke. Once I have the audio matched up with the video I'll evaluate once again if the joke is working.

- I try to include humor in my films that isn't reliant on being laugh out loud funny to work. Essentially, I am trying to write things that are not only funny but insightful, so even if the joke doesn't make someone laugh they will appreciate it on another level. The humor in my films typically falls into the categories of parody and satire, which have a deeper intent than simply being funny.

- It's funny to make fun of the fact that LEGO minifigures are made of plastic and can be taken apart and put back together. In *Parkour Battle* the characters can reassemble themselves if they break apart doing a dangerous trick. Essentially, it is good to embrace the fact that these characters and environments are made of plastic, and see where that takes you in regards to the humor.

- I think violence can be very funny with LEGO minifigures, due to their innocence. Their appearance seems contrary to violence, so it is inherently dissonant. In some of my older films I was somewhat looser with the laws of physics, which can be funny in a world of LEGO bricks.

Jonathan Vaughan has been creating LEGO stop-motion films, under his directorial name Nick Durron, since the summer of 2004 after discovering a fan-made trailer for *Star Wars Episode III*. His latest film, *Melting Point*, has been funded by a Kickstarter campaign that was backed by 180 people from all over the world.

© Jonathan Vaughan

What do you love most about making LEGO movies?

The thing I love most about brick-filming are the unlimited possibilities and total freedom it offers. I can essentially make a brick-film equivalent of a $150 million action movie for free. I don't have to worry about finding locations, costumes, actors, or any of the other challenges present in live-action filmmaking. Because of this, I think brick-filming is the absolute best way for young filmmakers to practice the craft of directing and learn the fundamentals of visual storytelling.

Another thing I love is being able to create something that is all my own work. I can design the sets, light the shots, position the camera, and animate it completely by myself. I have total creative control and don't have to worry about anyone else's ideas interfering with my creative vision.

***Zombie: Genesis* is one of your most popular videos, how did the idea for it come about?**

For whatever reason, I was thinking about what would happen on a movie set if a real zombie were

somehow there. I started saying out loud what the director might say about the situation in an interview. Bricks in Motion was hosting a contest the theme of which was "avant-garde." I had been planning not to enter and the deadline was only three weeks away, but with an idea this great I couldn't pass up the opportunity.

I wrote the script over two days. I included references to production challenges and stories I've heard about the making of real films. Obviously there was not much time to write the script, since I needed all the time remaining to make the film. I didn't storyboard it because I literally had every single shot in my head from the scripting stage. I did, however, write down a list of scenes—most of which were only a single shot—and would mark items off as I completed them, to help motivate myself.

The poster for *Zombie: Genesis*.
© Jonathan Vaughan

With only a few weeks to shoot, what was the hardest thing about the production stage?

One aspect of production that did prove difficult was assembling the voice cast. From the beginning I was always planning to voice the director. I was able to secure the voice actors playing the producer, the zombie wrangler, and the Swedish star quite easily; however, I had more difficulty with the rest of the cast because some of my friends were out of town or

otherwise unavailable. I recorded the last lines, those of Alex Rivers, on the morning of the day I needed to finish the film.

How did you find time to edit the film? Did you have to rush it all at the end?

I edited the film during production. Every day after I finished a scene or set of shots I would download them immediately and work on any visual effects needed for those shots, as well as add them into a master project where I began putting things in order and figuring out the timing. This enabled me to have the film nearly finished while shooting was still ongoing. The most significant visual effect in the film is the mouth animation. This was time consuming but not difficult as I'd used the same effect on several previous films. [Turn to page 175 for Jonathan's tutorial on moving mouths.]

Sound design has always been my least favorite part of the editing process, and as such I don't spend a great deal of time on it. I rely on free online sound effects libraries and a few sound packs I have for my resources. I rarely record my own sound effects.

Did you use any other effects that people might find interesting?

I used the plugin Twixtor for Adobe After Effects to slow down the zombie walk cycle. Filming slow movements with stop-motion is always very difficult, so being able to

adjust the speed of the zombies for added drama was incredibly useful. Essentially, what Twixtor does to slow down a shot is it creates new frames between the existing ones, instead of just fading between them. This results in a much more natural and fluid slow motion effect.

Zombies on the loose in *Zombie: Genesis*.
© Jonathan Vaughan

How was the film received?

The online reaction upon release was extremely positive. I was blown away. Most of my previous films had been criticized for their poorly developed stories and bad writing, but this film won over many of my harshest critics. Ultimately, the contest judges liked my film enough to give it first place. It was a great honor and pleasant surprise after rushing to complete the film in only three weeks.

***Zombie: Genesis* was shot with a Canon Powershot A640, and edited using Adobe Premiere Pro. Visual effects were created using Adobe After Effects. To watch the film and others by Jonathan Vaughan go to www.youtube.com/user/ NickDurron.**

7

EDITING AND ADDING EFFECTS

Yes, the rumors are true–you've finally finished shooting your stop-motion LEGO movie and you're ready to edit it into a finished production! After all those hours of animating, it might be tempting to throw all your shots into a sequence and be done with it, but the postproduction stage of brick-filming is essential for creating a polished product, so it's worth taking the extra time to really do your hard work justice. This is where you can put sound and visuals together, add in music, special effects, and titles, and remove anything that doesn't quite work. Even if you only spend a fraction of your production time on this stage, you'll be glad you did.

POSTPRODUCTION PROCESS

With stop-motion animation, the order you choose to get things done can be quite personal. Through trial and error you will come to learn the process that works for you. Some animators, for example, will record all of their soundtrack first—the sound that determines the length of their production, which might be dialogue or a song—and animate shot by shot using that soundtrack as a direct reference. This ensures they never capture more shots than they need. Other animators, however, will prefer to add dialogue in later or won't use dialogue at all, allowing their animating stage to be a little more relaxed. If your film requires lots of VFX sequences, if you're planning on animating your minifigures' mouths, or if you want to record your own sounds, all of these things will determine your postproduction process and the order you get things done.

For some, editing is the most painful part of the process, but for others it's where they finally see their animation come to life. "Editing is awesome," says Paul Hollingsworth. "When you're editing your own animation there's a sense of freedom to do anything." Paul animates using Dragonframe and then exports the takes as QuickTime movies. He then imports the footage into his editing software—Final Cut Pro—and adds the audio. "I concentrate on the dialogue first, and find the rhythm of the edit," he says. "Balancing action and comedy can be a challenge. I'll retime and adjust some of the frames of the animation if I have to." Any shots that require visual effects are then exported to After Effects. That's where he adds lasers and smoke and works on all the green screen shots. The footage is then returned to Final Cut Pro for fine-tuning.

In contrast, Chris Salt edits as he films. "As soon as the stop-motion is complete on a shot, I'll add it to the overall timeline to make sure it fits and works in context with everything else," he says. "Sets often get broken down and rebuilt from one shot to the next so it's important to make sure you're happy with what you have while it's all still intact. It also gives you an important sense of progress. When you're spending hours every day shooting frame after frame, you need that reassurance that what you're doing is building to something."

It's a good idea to think about the order you're going to do things so the process is smooth and efficient. Writing out the various stages in a suitable order and ticking them off as you go will help to keep the project moving.

Video editor Paul Hollingsworth spends his spare time making epic action films with LEGO. Some of his most popular productions include well-known characters from big studio franchises, scaled down to great effect.

When did you first start dabbling in LEGO stop-motion?

After graduating from film school, I worked as an editor on TV shows and low-budget movies, but any chance I could get I would make my own movies. I dusted off my old LEGO and recreated an epic *Braveheart*-style attack on a castle. That film went on to win at Brickfest in 2002. When I went to the convention I was amazed to see it play on the large screen in front of an audience of over 200 people.

How did you come to be part of Digital Wizards Studios?

I read online about a brick-filming competition in Colorado, but the deadline was in ten days, and a writer/editor buddy, Steve Banta, said, "It would be cool to see what we could do in ten days." Challenge accepted. We shot a LEGO version of *Cowboys & Aliens*. . . . My friend David Kelly at Voodoo Highway agreed to give us a professional mix . . . That first brick-film was how we formed Digital Wizards. We made thirteen more films over the next year.

And what does your daughter, Hailee, think about the hobby?

She has lots of ideas about which minifigs, accessories, and props to use. Her creativity has helped me gain perspective. Since it takes a while to set up the lights and the background, Hailee will play with the characters and that often sparks certain movements and ideas. She even hangs out in the studio to help animate scenes.

Hailee has her own show called *BrickGirl*. She'll build a LEGO kit and review it. Recently

Scenes from Digital Wizards' *LEGO Avengers: Some Assembly Required.*
© Paul Hollingsworth

Hailee Hollingsworth, Brick Girl on YouTube, making movie magic on the set of Digital Wizards' *LEGO Superman vs. Sharknado.*
© Paul Hollingsworth

we started animating minifigs building the kits. It's a fun way to play with the characters and simultaneously build a kit. It makes it possible to see the immediate gratification of stop-motion animation.

A lot of your films use characters from licensed LEGO themes—what is the key to making these films different from the film/TV characters audiences know?

Everything that we create is a parody. I enjoy taking beloved characters and exploring a different side of them, playing with a character's strengths and weaknesses—whether it's an overconfident millionaire Tony Stark arguing with Jarvis or Batman's choice of a soy latte at Starbucks.

Why did you decide to make an Avengers film?

When I saw *The Avengers* in the theater I was blown away. Here were characters I've loved in comics and cartoons brought to life on screen in a very realistic way. I was still in the middle of a four-month shoot for another film but I knew that I had to make a LEGO Avengers brick-film. I went out and purchased all the LEGO Avengers kits immediately.

It was only a week later my wife and I were on vacation in New York City and we ran into Mark Ruffalo [who plays Bruce Banner/The Hulk] on Park Ave. at a hot dog stand. While there I took a lot of inspiration from the architecture, the cramped skyscrapers,

the Brooklyn Bridge, Statue of Liberty. I wrote the first draft of script on the plane ride back to LA and developed it over the next two months.

Were there any major challenges that you faced?

Storyboarding was important because there were so many visual effects. Almost every scene needed compositing, green screen, rotoscoping, facial animation. . . . It was a huge undertaking for us to crank that out in our spare time in six weeks.

I have what I thought was a pretty large LEGO collection but I don't have everything. I had a lot of support from friends through LUGOLA [LEGO User Group of Los Angeles]. When I built the Brooklyn Bridge, I thought it looked huge and then when I filmed it with cars on it, I couldn't help but think how small it looked. Whoops! That was an important lesson—sense of scale is very important.

The green screen footage was intense; one of the trickiest shots was Leviathan. I had a pico dolly—it's like a little skateboard on wheels—to set the camera on; we were filming a 90-degree spin around it. Rigging a creature or flying ship is always tricky. You want to make sure that the points you attach to aren't interfering with or blocking the model, and a lot of the shadows had to be rotoscoped out. It was very time consuming, but sometimes that's the only solution.

Were there any new or interesting techniques you used in the making of the film?

We've been developing our facial animations since day one. I would rather see mouths move; that's how we treat brick-filming—like a professional animation. Imagine going to see a Pixar or Disney animation and the mouths not moving? Moving mouths and great voice acting helps the audience identify and relate to all your characters.

At first we had basic mouth moves, but then we started drawing more mouths and faces and finding ways to track them onto the heads. By *Avengers* we had a great system for sync where we shoot a blank LEGO face and then add the facial animation on top of it. It's gotten easier the more we do it, but it still is very time intensive. [For more on this technique turn to page 167.]

Your films involve quite a lot of visual effects. Which are you most proud of?

Currently I've been working on a Superman brick-film that is deep in FX. I've been trying to push the limits of my motion control setup. I have an OmniSlider with an eMotimo motion control head. It hooks up directly to Dragonframe and can be controlled to dolly, pan, and tilt. Through Dragonframe you can do multiple passes of the same camera moves. So I film a clean plate of the background. And then shoot another take of Superman or Zod or a spaceship attached to a rig. That way, when it gets to After Effects it's easy to rotoscope the rigging and have a clean plate.

So much of stop-motion is the photography of the shot, everything can exist in that same environment. The trick to any visual effect is to not have it stand out. If the audience notices it, it's a failure. Blending the effects so they don't stand out is a balancing act.

What has been the online reaction to *LEGO Avengers: Some Assembly Required*?

It recently hit over a million views on YouTube and has had a very positive reaction online. Comic fans love it; LEGO fans love it. It's a funny script with a blend of action and comedy, some rare LEGO kits that are hard to find, lots of pop-culture references, and some huge scenes, which many brick-filmers don't attempt.

Watch this film and more from Paul Hollingsworth and the Digital Wizards team at www .digitalwizards.tv

Photos © Paul Hollingsworth

ADDING AUDIO

When to record or source audio for your film really depends on your process. If you have a dialogue-heavy film, it might make sense to create an audio track prior to beginning your animation so you have a good idea of how long each shot needs to be to fit in all the talking. This could be a rough recording, used simply for timing. If you would like to animate to a particular piece of music or audio clip from another source, then having this already sitting in your editing timeline will enable you to hit all the right notes with your animation, and might actually inspire it. For additional sound effects and a musical score, it might make more sense to shoot the animation first and then add in the appropriate sounds and music that work with what you've created.

"The visuals are only half the story," says David Boddy. "Never underestimate the power that sound brings." And he's quite right. The addition of any sound element—be it a music soundtrack, dialogue, or movement-specific sound effects, like the noise of your minifigure's feet walking on a tiled floor or the burning crackle of a fire—can completely transform your film, altering the audience's perception, building suspense, driving narrative, and injecting comedy. Of course it's up to you what sound you include—a silent movie could include subtitles, for example—but if you're willing to give it a go there's a lot of fun to be had both for you and the audience.

- If you want to hear what your characters have to say then you're going to need to record that dialogue yourself. Turn to page 160 for voice-acting tips.

- Most cartoons use sound effects with great results. Watch some of your favorite cartoons to get an idea of when and how these are added and to what effect.

- There are many websites that have a range of free music and sound effects you can use without paying the copyright holder. See the resources section on page 199. Some stipulate a specific notice or link should be included somewhere noticeably in your film's credits.

- Always be conscious of the intended audience of your films—are you just going to screen them to friends and family at home or are you planning on posting them online? If they are going to be made public, you should respect any copyright of the sounds you're using. If you're unsure of who the copyright holder is, make every effort to find out. If you think you might be breaching someone's copyright, find an alternative solution.

- Recording your own sound effects is the easiest way to avoid copyright confusion. Everything around you can be used to create sounds for your films from the ordinary—recording *yourself* walking—to the more unusual. When David Boddy couldn't find a sound he liked for a spider running, he recorded a pair of scissors opening and closing and adjusted the pitch to use in his film.

Voice acting

Great animation will bring your characters to life, and some of the best examples of stop-motion animation show that often characters don't even need to talk to convey personality and emotions. Their body language, expressions, timing, and the way you cut the frames together can provide enough narrative for the audience to understand your characters and their relationship to one another without anyone saying a word. Sometimes, however, well-written dialogue and some clever voice acting is exactly what your film requires to make it shine.

Focus on Foley

Zach Macias of MindGame Studios spends a lot of time designing the sound for his films—going so far as to record his own ambient sounds and adding them in postproduction to enhance the audio quality and believability of a scene—a commonly used craft in the film industry known as "foley." For him this stage is the most involving part of making a stop-motion film after the animation itself. "I am a big advocate for proper sound design," he says. "I've seen far too many potentially great brick-films fall flat on their face because of poor sound editing. What you see on screen is only half of the effect—the sound of something has just as much personality as the visual." For his film *Stranger than Fishin'*, which features a man fishing on a dock, he recorded a lot of the sounds himself. "I was very particular about how I wanted things to sound," he says, "especially the fidelity of different objects on different surfaces. I didn't want the foley mix to overpower the music, but certain actions required a certain 'impact' that the music alone couldn't provide. Sometimes, it's also a matter of filling in the 'gaps' to keep the pacing consistent."

Recording your own sound can be a fun and rewarding experience, but where experimentation is concerned perfection can be elusive, so learn to work with what you've got and if that means recreating the sounds of an ocean in your bathroom, go for it!

Acting might not be your forte, but if you're keen to master this one-man movie machine process, then you can give it a go in the privacy of your own home, without an audience. And the good news is, once the film is uploaded, no one will know that it's your voice anyway. By performing your script out loud you'll have a better understanding of what works and what doesn't. Someone who knows how to morph into multiple characters is Digital Wizards' Paul Hollingsworth. And these are his top tips.

- Voice-over recording is by far one of my favorite stages of filmmaking. Brick-films are small cartoons so I treat it whimsically. It's LEGO—it's a toy! It's fun and cute by nature.
- The most basic equipment you will need to record audio is a microphone and some kind of recorder. It doesn't need to be anything expensive—some people record on their phones.
- If you have a bit more cash to spare and want to improve the quality of your sound, Blue Yeti has a great USB mic, which runs about $80– $140 and plugs right into your computer. It makes it really easy to record.
- Try to find the quietest environment in your house to record. Not everyone has access to a sound booth, but you can mock up one with a little resourcefulness. Hang blankets behind you and on the opposite side of the microphone. It will help reduce audio reverberation.
- Creating voices is great fun. As a video editor, I hear voices all day from footage I'm cutting, interviews, movies, trailers, and so on. I imitate, and experiment with voices constantly.

Try talking back to the computers and movies, try accents, try new characters, try finding a characteristic of someone's voice and exploit it for comedy.

- Although you might be shy, voice-over sessions are best if you collaborate. A script is just words on a page until an actor brings it to life. Working with others brings fresh perspectives to your ideas.
- Sometimes you have to let go and try to get rid of any inhibitions. I've come up with a couple of voice characters that are just ridiculous, but would never have gotten there if I didn't push my limits. Don't be afraid of trying something new. Don't worry about sounding silly or stupid.
- When voice acting, it's important to put yourself into character. I like to stand up, stay loose and try a few lines in character voice as a lead into the lines in a script.
- For someone new to voicing I would recommend practicing. Record yourself and play it back. Always record multiple takes, pick the best ones, and then cut those in to your finished film.
- We improvise in the voice-over booth a lot. We may listen to clips of an existing character, but that is only a jumping off point. We want to develop the character's unique sound. My personal preference is to not do a completely accurate sounding imitation, but to find a cartoonier version.
- If your film involves multiple characters, but you don't have any willing friends to make the characters sound different, use your own voice

in imaginative ways when you record them—maybe one character has an accent of speaks in a different register. Maybe they slur, or are always angry. You can then lower or raise the pitch, play with EQ [equalization], compressors, and reverb to make further changes.

Don't want to release your inner movie star? Then why not ask others to do the voices for you? David Boddy says his films really benefit from using other people's voices. "Variety makes it sound much better," he says. "In my film *Cyclic* I spent a lot of time on the script. I had other people read it and make suggestions. We have a small sound booth where I work. I auditioned a dozen colleagues using a line or two from the script. There were several stand-outs, who I then had read the full script for the character I thought they suited. It made such a difference to the feel of the film. Even those that sounded amateurish added a charming quality that my voice, even when digitally modified, didn't."

EDITING SOFTWARE

There are many options when it comes to editing. You can use a professional editing system, a standard editing system or free software, or even edit on your phone or tablet. Spending money on a professional suite is a big commitment, so if you are thinking of buying Final Cut Pro or Adobe Premiere Pro, for example, make sure you're committed to filmmaking as a hobby so you know you're going to get the most use out of the software (editing software can be used for stop-motion and all other kinds of filmmaking too). If you're less sure about where your stop-motion journey is going to take you, it's advisable to try things out using a more basic program, which will allow you to practice editing techniques but might be restrictive in other ways. Preinstalled movie editing systems are designed to simplify the process. If your editing software is not up to the task, you can usually download trial versions of more advanced software for free.

The three main elements of any video editing software will be:

- Library—this is where you can keep track of and access all the media you upload to the project. From the library you can drag and drop elements into your timeline/clip sequencer.
- Timeline/clip sequencer—this is where you line up all your sequences in the order you want and edit them together with audio and any effects. Some basic software may only have a storyboard/clip sequencer rather than a timeline interface. The latter gives you more control and allows you to cut sequences/audio tracks up and move them around the timeline as you see fit.
- Preview window—this is where you can see your film taking shape as you edit. Most software allows you to move through a sequence frame by frame or play back between certain points.

Once you've identified the main components of your software, you can start to edit by opening a new project and importing media from wherever you've stored your animation sequences. You can then drag and drop a series of frames into the timeline and start to move them around, make cuts, or change the length of certain shots. Your software will probably have many other capabilities such as using multiple video and audio layers, as well as adding in effects, transitions, and fades. If you're having trouble understanding your particular software, check out the manufacturer's website for video tutorials or search online for stop-motion specific help—the Internet provides a wealth of simple how-to videos for a variety of pro and basic software.

Editing tips

No matter what software you are choosing to slice your film into shape with, these tips to editing excellence should keep you on track.

- Be organized! Editing requires the level of efficient organization discussed earlier with regards to animating. If you labeled all your shots in your storyboard and shot list, and sorted these sequences into labeled folders for import, you will find it a lot easier to piece your film back together, no matter what order you filmed it in.
- Experiment with the different kinds of cuts or transitions your software offers. The main types are straight cuts, where you cut back and forth between scenes or characters; dissolves, where one shot merges into the next; and fade-outs or fade-ins, where the shot gradually appears from a black screen or fades out to a black screen. Your software will probably offer lots of different options, which can be used to great effect.
- Unless you're going for a disorienting, fast-paced feel, try to avoid fast-cutting your shots. If you've not taken enough frames for a particular shot and the action is too fast, you can increase the length of certain frames or the whole sequence. Cutting back and forth too rapidly between characters or cutting too quickly from wide shots to close-ups will be noticeable and annoying for the viewer.
- Great editing is never really noticed by the audience. The pacing and movement from one shot to the next should feel natural. One way to disrupt that illusion is with continuity mistakes. Something as small as showing a character wearing a hat in one shot and then it disappearing with no explanation in the next will stand out and become the audience's focus, rather than the action you've worked so hard to capture.

CREATING EFFECTS

In-camera effects can look great, but there are some things it might be harder or impossible to achieve in this way. Some effects can be achieved using your editing software, but for more complex visual effects it might be worth using a program such as Adobe After Effects, which is designed specifically for creating motion graphics and video compositing. There are also other options such as Wax 2.0 and HitFilm 2 Ultimate, which you can trial for free. Depending on the software available to you and the amount of time you want to spend, there are a whole host of exciting effects you can create to add visual interest to your film. A sign of a good visual effect is when the audience cannot tell how it was achieved, and question whether it was added using a computer program or by the animator on the set. To this end, in general it's best not to overuse them, but rather allow them to complement your animation.

Camera moves in postproduction

You can create the illusion of camera moves in postproduction using a program such as After Effects to "move" the whole static camera sequence around the screen. If you are using digital stills, the camera's "native" images will be much larger than any standard video sizes anyway. This means that there is lots of leeway to move around and zoom into the image without losing picture quality. While camera exports will vary, most output an image *much* bigger than even full Blu-ray size. You can therefore compose your shots for some dramatic camera moves. If you are capturing from video, your image will already be one of the standard video frame sizes. In this case you will be losing quality if you zoom into the image to move it about the screen, so your option will be more limited. Zooming in somewhere between 103 percent and 110 percent will probably pass unnoticed by the viewer, though, which will allow you to create a handheld drift effect. And in some cases you might be able to zoom in as far as 140 percent before the image becomes too pixilated.

Explosions

Dynamic explosions are full of movement and color, and can bring your action scenes to life. Paul Hollingsworth explains how he creates LEGO explosions in After Effects.

- "An explosion is most effective when it's story based. It has to mean something. In *The Lord of the Rings*, Saruman's orcs blow up the wall and can now get through and slaughter the Rohan army. In *Star Wars* they are used to demonstrate the power of the Death Star and then to defeat the Death Star. I like using explosions towards the climax of the movie."

- "When I'm filming an explosion, I like to add an additional light for a few frames. I ramp up the brightness over the course of three or four frames and get to its brightest, and then bring it down again. I cover that light with a red or orange gel. A built in lighting effect will help to sell your visual effect."

- "If you are compositing, always shoot a background plate—an image of your background without any moving elements in the foreground. It must be the exact same angle and focal distance as your shot. I also like to shoot LEGO pieces of the elements like a broken building or section of a wall, bricks, minfigs, debris; these are great for rotoscoping and layering them on top of the explosion we'll use in After Effects."

Digital Wizards' epic Helm's Deep explosion from *LEGO Lord of the Rings: Two Towers in Two Minutes*.
© Paul Hollingsworth

Using After Effects, or a similar software, follow Paul's step-by-step guide to creating explosions.
1. Add your background plate into your composition.
2. Add your shot layer over the top.
3. Add your explosion over that. Make sure the alpha channel is set correctly. You don't want the ugly black lines as it looks sloppy. Experiment with the composite mode you like—I like Add, Screen, or Multiply. Sometimes I will copy explosions and layer them over each other with different composite modes.
4. Add any of your elements over that.
5. Rotoscope any of the rigs, elements, and debris.
6. Set all motion paths for the flying elements and add motion blur.
7. Add a camera shake or lens flare or both (optional).

Real Explosions

It's not advisable to blow up your LEGO for real, as durable as it is. But some compressed air and a rickety structure can make for explosive effects. For *LEGO Lord of the Rings: Two Towers in Two Minutes* the Digital Wizards team shot the Helm's Deep wall being destroyed in live action. "We built a loose version of the wall with the bricks just lightly being held together," says Paul Hollingsworth. A can of compressed air was then used to shoot at the wall and send the bricks flying all over the place. "Shooting live could be considered 'a cheat,'" says Paul, "but it is also one of the only ways to film realistic smoke. If the shot looks good, why not? Other elements like bricks and minifigs were layered over the explosion in post and sent scattering in different directions."

Making mouths move

LEGO minifigures were created as a simple people—originally they were available with one smiling facial expression, and they stayed that way for many years. The launch of the LEGO Pirates theme in 1989 saw the introduction of minifigures with different facial features—beards, hair, eye patches, etc.—a new direction that was developed in subsequent 1990s themes. More recently, the launch of the collectible minifigure series has introduced even more elaborate characters, expressions, hats, and hairpieces, making it easier than ever before to bring that variety to your films.

Anyone who's used to watching traditional 2D animations and 3D animations, has an expectation that the characters' mouths will move in line with their voices. It is possible to achieve this with LEGO minifigures using visual effects. "Mouth animation in a brick-film makes the characters come alive and feel real," says Jonathan Vaughan. "It also adds a great deal more emotion to the characters. LEGO minifigures are so static and, barring a few exceptions, only have one facial expression. Adding mouth animation helps the voice of the actor connect with the image onscreen. It is also very impressive technically, because viewers know that it is a visual effect. I endeavor to make the effect perfectly seamless, so there are no signs of compositing or trickery. Hopefully this makes some viewers question for a moment if the effect was in fact achieved in camera somehow."

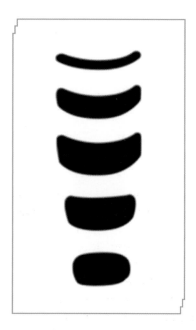

Different LEGO mouths for a variety of phonetic shapes can be downloaded online or create your own.
© Jonathan Vaughan

Director's Chair
Zach Boivin

Zach Boivin started dabbling in stop-motion in 2007, and now produces super-slick videos. He has even produced films for LEGO, including *The Gold Getaway*, which incorporates some great visual effects and a rather impressive explosion scene.

How were you inspired to start making brick-films?

In 2007, LEGO held a brick-filming contest. Although I didn't enter, I watched the winners and was inspired to create my own films. I made a few animations with a camcorder, but didn't really get into it at first. Three years later, my parents got me a book on brick-filming; that's when I started making YouTube videos. My inspiration comes from just about everywhere. Usually from movies, videogames, music, books, or other brick-films.

What do you love about the medium?

I like that you have the power to turn any idea into a video. You create your own world where anything is possible.

***The Gold Getaway* is one of your most popular videos, and includes a number of visual effects. How much planning went into it?**

I usually come up with an idea, summarize it into a shot list, then build from there. Since *The Gold Getaway* didn't have any dialogue, I decided to skip the script and move right on to storyboarding. I shot the film within the period of about a month.

What was the largest set you built? And how many trees did you use for your forest?

Measuring in at about five feet long, the largest set I used was the bridge scene. It took up most of my table and was too large for my blue-screen to completely cover the background. No more than forty trees where used in any given shot. Any more you see are just pasted in using After Effects (see the next page).

How do you go about animating such a complex action-based film?

I look at my storyboards and start shooting the scenes in order of location. I animated the whole film at 15fps. When I'm done with a scene, I save the video to my computer and move onto the next shot. At first, I wasn't 100 percent sure how I would end the film. I just started filming and came up with the idea to add the monkey halfway. I was so happy I did!

© Zach Boivin

The LEGO forest set from *The Gold Getaway*.
© Zach Boivin

by taking elements from Action Essentials 2 and compositing them together on top of the animation.

How did you create the visual effect of the trees rushing past the cars?

All the trees you see passing in front of the camera were done in post. I took pictures of a bunch of trees in front of a blue screen so I could key them out and use them for any scenes that needed more trees. I used After Effects to animate still pictures of trees passing by really fast—two to three frames. I added motion blur to create the sense of motion.

Are there special effects you used that you're particularly proud of?

Near the beginning of the film I wanted to make a cool effect where the camera moved underground to reveal the cave below; this was something I had never done before. To accomplish this, I had to build my set as a two-story cross-section. The transition was done by adjusting my tripod so that the camera would move down slightly every frame until it reached the bottom.

What does your postproduction process entail?

After the animation is done, I finish off my clips in After Effects. Explosions, lens flares, masking, chroma keying, and all the cool effects are done here. When that's done, I open Premiere Pro and start editing. I add sound effects, music, and color correction to all my clips until it's ready to render.

What visual effect are you most proud of?

The effect I'm most proud of is the explosion scene near the end. I love how the matte painting turned out in this shot. The explosion was one of my favorite effects to work on—it's not every day I get to blow up a bridge! I built some of the set, but the rest was blue-screen. I composited pictures of the cliff that were shot at different angles to make the background. Trees were also added along with the sky and clouds. The explosion was made

What's been the online reaction to the film?

It's received hundreds of thousands of views on YouTube along with a lot of positive feedback. I work hard on my videos so it's awesome to see them getting a lot of views. I read all the comments and use the feedback to improve my content.

***The Gold Getaway* was shot using a Logitech C920 webcam with a LEGO-built rig. Zach animates using The Helium Frog Animator, adds visual effects using Adobe After Effects and Action Essentials 2, and edits with Premiere Pro. To watch the film and others from Zach Boivin go to www.youtube .com/user/ZachFBStudios.**

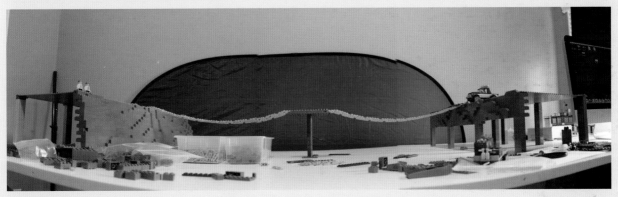

The large bridge explosion set and the finished scene after visual effects.
© Zach Boivin

Follow Jonathan Vaughan's step-by-step guide to achieving moving minifigure mouths. The pictures and captions refer to how to achieve the process in After Effects, but these stages below can be applied to other software.

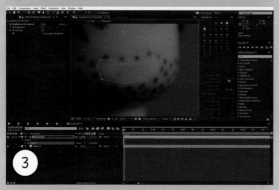

1. To begin with, I always shoot my characters with a regular LEGO face. It is possible to film with a blank face and completely add a new one in postproduction, but this is much more time-consuming and doesn't look any better, in my opinion.

2. In postproduction, I begin by taking a single frame from the shot and painting out the existing mouth on the LEGO character. This is done using the clone stamp tool.

3. I then draw a mask to isolate the painted-out mouth region and motion track this to the character's face over the course of the shot.

4. Now that the original mouth is gone, I create a new one. This is done by drawing a mask on a solid black layer in the shape of the mouth.

5. Next I key-frame the mask on this layer and make phonemes. Phonemes are the different shapes a person's mouth makes as they say different letters. Typically I make five: closed mouth, consonants (l, m, s, etc.), a wide open mouth (a), a slightly open mouth (e, i, u), and a circular mouth (o, r, w).

6. Next I move through the shot frame by frame while listening to the audio, and copy the appropriate phoneme needed at each point. After I've finished I watch the shot through and adjust anything that doesn't look right.

7. Finally, I track the new mouth to match the movement of the LEGO character's face and do any additional compositing needed to make the effect look real. For example, if a light streak falls on the character's face at one point, I need to add the streak in the right spot on the new mouth. All told, this process takes one to two hours per shot, regardless of length.

(7)

Photos © Jonathan Vaughan

Jonathan uses Adobe After Effects for this process but other software with similar capabilities might also be suitable. "This effect could also be achieved in any image editing program such as Adobe Photoshop or GIMP," says Jonathan. "However, it will take a great deal more time as the effect would need to be applied to every frame individually. An alternative method that might work better in these programs is to warp the existing mouth on the LEGO character into different shapes. This would eliminate the need to paint out the original mouth and create a new one. I actually used this method for one shot in *Zombie: Genesis*. It is useful at times, but in my experience does not work often due to the risk of warping unwanted areas of the shot around the mouth."

Before and after warping a character's mouth in *Zombie: Genesis* by Jonathan Vaughan.
© Jonathan Vaughan

Many brick-films don't use visual effects to create moving mouths to match dialogue—some animators choose to switch in different heads to show strong emotions instead or purchase identical copies of the LEGO head and draw in different mouth shapes using a marker, but Jonathan warns against relying on this method for more than a couple of shots. "During filming, you would need to swap out the head every frame for the one with the appropriate shape, using the recording of the actor's voice as a reference for timing," he says. "This method allows much less flexibility and it would be difficult to keep the character from moving in unwanted ways while removing and replacing the head for every frame."

Lindsay Fleay drew different expressions on blank heads and switched them in and out to create his characters' varied reactions in *The Magic Portal*.
© Lindsay Fleay

PROFESSIONAL FINISH

While a short film might be fine without a title card and credits, it's a great way to set the tone and present your work professionally. No need to go overboard, but a simple introductory sequence that tells the audience the film's title in a suitable font is a good idea. This can tie in with any promotional materials you might create such as a movie poster to share on your social media channels or website. A credit sequence at the end of the film is a clean way to mark the end. It lets the audience know that you directed it, which gets your name out there, and it's also the appropriate place to thank and acknowledge others who have contributed to your film, whether as voice actors, fellow animators, or by lending you their LEGO. If you have used any audio or visual effects that should be credited, then include these too. A lot of brickfilmmakers round up the end of their film with links to their other works or website; this is a really simple way of driving traffic to your films and increasing your audience.

8
UPLOADING AND PROMOTING YOUR FILMS

Grab the popcorn and dim the lights, it's time to sit back, relax, and watch your movie on the big screen (if you have one). Alternatively, you can watch it on a small screen, and share it with millions of other people and their small screens around the world. After what might have been months of hard work, presenting your movie to the public can be a little overwhelming. *What will people say? What if I'm the only person who thinks it's any good? What if nobody watches it?* These are the thoughts that run through the minds of most creative people on the precipice of publication, but you needn't fear. Sharing your film doesn't have to involve the whole world and their tactless commentary. And if you do choose to submit your work to the hungry mouths of YouTube viewers, you might find some of the feedback helpful, motivating, and confidence boosting, spurring you on to make even better films. This chapter aims to make the prospect of uploading and sharing a little less daunting.

UPLOADING

Some brick-filmmakers choose to post their videos exclusively on their own website, but the vast majority use free public sites like YouTube and Vimeo to upload their videos. These sites are easy to use and provide an instant audience for your films. As most of you will be familiar with YouTube, and as this is the most popular website for watching and uploading brick-films, the following information is largely tailored to those choosing to use it as their primary platform, although most of the principles can be applied to other sites.

Video formats

When you export your film from your editing software, you can select the appropriate settings for its destination, whether that be YouTube or to a DVD. At a glance, the world of video formats is very confusing, but when it comes to knowing which format to export your film in, there are only a few things you need to pay attention to. A video format is made up of two components—containers and codecs. It makes sense to think of the container as the structure of the file itself and the codec as its contents. The container is usually identified by its file extension (e.g., .AVI or .MP4).

A good container can use multiple codecs, which compress films to make them more manageable for our computers. YouTube states that the best format to use for the best playback results is a MP4 container with one of the following codecs: H.264, MPEG-2, or MPEG-4. The great thing about this site is that it has the ability to support different formats, and automatically optimizes your films for online playback.

Audio formats

Don't forget about your sound—its quality is equally important to your audience's enjoyment of your video. YouTube recommends you encode your sound in AAC-LC format, using Stereo and a sample rate of 96khz or 48khz.

Frames rate

Remember to export your film with the same fps rate that you shot it in when you're uploading to the Internet. If you're exporting to watch the film on TV or for DVD viewing, the settings will depend on where you are in the world. You should use the format and settings you would normally use to export nonanimated video. Don't worry, this won't affect the frame rate you used while animating—the software will correctly interpret the difference.

Resolution

This refers to the number of pixels that are used in each image of the video—the more pixels, the higher the definition and the sharper the picture. It's a good idea to upload your videos in high definition so audiences with larger monitors will be able to enjoy them at a high quality too.

Aspect ratio

YouTube adjusts all videos to fit the aspect ratio of its viewer window—16:9. If you've used that aspect ratio your film will fit precisely in the viewer, but if you've adjusted your movie to a 4:3 aspect ratio, then YouTube will automatically add vertical black bars on either side of the image so it fits the viewing window without stretching the picture. Don't add your own letterbox bars onto a 4:3 video to try and make it fit the viewer, because then you will end up with bars on all sides.

With your video uploaded, YouTube gives you the option to make it public or private, choose a thumbnail to represent the video—it's a good idea to use your title page here, or a great close-up that will really sell the film if people stumble across it while browsing—and add additional audio, captions, and annotations, such as links to subscribe to your channel or visit your website.

Private Screening

Don't feel up to the anonymous gaze of thousands of online viewers? Another great way to get feedback and share your hard work is to organize a screening for friends and family. Ask around for friends with digital projectors and invite people to watch a movie, then make your film the preview as a surprise! For a bigger audience, try asking your local multiplex if they can show it, or enter local film festivals.

PROMOTING YOUR FILMS

"It's easy to lose sight of views and viewership on a place like YouTube, where a large number of creators are able to pull in millions and millions of views on average per video," says Zach Macias. "For a guy like me, who pretty much has been doing this on his own on a desk in his bedroom since he was a teenager, to have more than one video in the million views club is really quite an honor, one that goes well beyond what I imagined years ago." This is an important point to keep in mind, because once your films are uploaded, you might be wondering why you and your mom/best friend/partner are the only people viewing them, when "everyone else" seems to be wowing audiences of millions.

There are *a lot* of videos online, and brick-filmmaking is a popular hobby. Some animators have been doing this for years and have the catalog of films and number of views to prove it. While there is always the chance a film you make will "get lucky" and go viral among brick-filmmakers and the wider YouTube audience, promoting them is a more predictable way of helping to get your work the attention it deserves. Here are some simple ideas to get you started.

- Publicize your videos. If you have a website or are part of any forums, clubs, or social networking sites, don't shy away from self-promotion. Send out an e-newsletter to all your friends and family with links to new videos—being direct and personal is a surefire way to encourage people to click. Always ask others to subscribe to your channel and to share, like, and comment on anything you post, as this will help spread the post further.
- Give your films interesting and eye-catching titles. "LEGO Star Wars brick-film" generates nearly 50,000 results on YouTube's search engine. Chris Salt says, "Everyone loves Star Wars so a Star Wars brick-film probably seems like a good idea when you're starting out. It sounds like a good idea to everyone though. It's important to make something that stands out too."
- Don't forget to add tags to the video that will optimize its position in any search.
- Create YouTube badges for your website so you are constantly driving traffic to your channel.
- Build a following on Twitter by following as many LEGO fans, brick-film fans, and

animation fans as possible. Always include a link to your latest video in any tweets.

- Don't be sloppy when uploading videos. Make sure you always include a description with any interesting information, including technical specs. Always add a subscription link or banner and links to any how-to videos or related videos at the end of your film. The description is a great place to include links to behind-the-scenes photos on Flickr or another photo-sharing website. This way you're encouraging the audience to spend more time clicking around your channel.

- Enable comments on your videos. If you don't then you are denying the audience the chance to engage with your channel. Yes, you might receive some negative feedback, but the comments allows you to respond to technical queries and communicate with your audience.

- Once you've built up a collection of videos, it's wise to create playlists, collating videos by theme or type. Some animators will group all their Star Wars videos together, for example, or all their "how-to" films.

- Another great way to generate traffic is to announce a contest or challenge on your page.

This might not have to involve giving away a prize (although that always helps), but could be a fun and clever contest to inspire other LEGO fans.

All this aside, Zach Macias says that the best advice he can give to new animators is not to have your goals set on the outcome, but rather on the product. "There are dozens of ways to properly 'promote' your video but that can only take you so far," he says. "Firstly, and most importantly, you have to produce something that people will want to watch. Put more thought, energy, and worry into the actual production of your film—teach yourself everything you need to and spend as much time as required to make your final product as close to your vision as you can. A quickly-thrown together parody of the most recent Internet trend may secure you some views while it's still popular, but once that fad passes, so will interest in your product. To make something that you're truly passionate about, and if that passion is clearly seen in the final film, then that, at the very least, has the potential to live on far longer."

Daniel Utecht has been messing around with LEGO and cameras since he was a child. He's known for his YouTube hit *The Dandelion,* which has received over four million views on the site.

When did you start making LEGO animations?

When I was around ten, me and some neighbors, started making little animations with a video camera, but it was nothing like what I do now. In 2009 I watched *Jericho: A Promise Fulfilled* at the San Antonio Independent Christian Film Festival and it was amazing. I started looking around and bought a DSLR camera and some animation software.

Some people spend months making their films. Is there something more exciting about the fact you can do something really quickly with LEGO?

I have kind of a short attention span in that if I come up with a really good idea I think about it continuously, so after a few weeks if I haven't started working on it I can get tired of the idea. I'm more of the type of person who likes to work on a film really hard for a few weeks and bang the film out.

***The Dandelion* is a great example of a simple idea that is highly effective–and the dialogue-free action is a great style of film for new animators to try and emulate. How did you come up with it?**

I was on a walk with my mom and she said, "Why don't you do something with dandelions?" I work for several of my neighbors during the summer mowing yards, pulling weeds, [and] dealing with dandelions, so I have an understanding of the frustration of the difficulty that can come with trying to get rid of these things, so it kind of sprouted from that. I create the story as I make the film so I just started filming. I found that music piece that kicks in after about one minute, and then I thought I would sync the animation with it, showing his increasingly drastic measures to get rid of the dandelion.

The title card for Daniel Utecht's film *The Dandelion.*
© Daniel Utecht

© Daniel Utecht

Do you think for a beginner, making a film to a piece of music is a good idea because there is an existing framework to begin with?

Yeah. Some people might think it's easier to have dialogue in their film. I'm more of a structured person so I think having music to structure my animations around makes it easier for me. If it's your very first animation, you might want to just do animation without sound just to get the feel of how it works. You kind of build each step of the way. You start with the basics and then you add in a new thing like sound effects, music, special effects, different movements with the minifigure, etc.

What part of the film are you most proud of, and how did you achieve it?

There were quite a few things when I made the movie where I wasn't sure what to do. Being new to animating, I would actually Google and then look for other people's ways of doing it and adapt it for my own use. I completed the whole film—I was amazed at how long it was—and since I already had the set I thought I might as well do something else for the end. I decided to have the words 'The End' made from LEGO, scroll onto the screen, then they tilted one way, then they tilted back, and they kind of rocked like it was really moving.

For the bit where the screen fills with smoke I used cotton balls. I had the car start to spin back and forth, that's where I started putting cotton balls in the screen, and I just put more and more cotton balls for each shot, and then once the screen was full of cotton balls, using the Pinnacle Studio program I put a video file of smoke. And then when the smoke clears there's no cotton balls.

What it's been like to get such a huge response on YouTube?

I had no idea it would be this popular. It was my second main film. My first had gotten some attention, it probably had ten to twenty thousand views at the time, and I thought even that was quite a lot. When I released *The Dandelion,* it didn't get a ton of attention right away and then all of a sudden, boom! I was getting thousands of views each day. I didn't do anything. I just uploaded it, and it's still getting so many.

The Dandelion was shot using a Canon Rebel XSi. Daniel uses AnimatorHD to capture, GIMP to edit photos, and Sony Vegas to edit his videos. To see this film and more, go to www.youtube .com/user/FilmsByDan.

LEGO words "The End" zip onto the screen with ease.
© Daniel Utecht

Go with What They Know

If you want to generate views on your YouTube channel or direct traffic to your site, one way to encourage hits is to make a video using a theme that is already well-established in popular culture, or something "of the moment" that's likely to attract attention—a LEGO music video of a recent hit song or a parody of a popular TV show. If generating views is all you're interested in then these types of videos can be very popular, but if you want to develop into a skilled animator, you're better off taking your time to be original, as David Boddy explains. "A popular YouTube video does not always mean a good one. Remakes of existing work don't interest me at all even though they can be successful in finding an audience and generating a lot of views. If a movie like *Batman* is made shot for shot as a LEGO brick-film it will never be as good as the original. I understand many do this to learn more about the process, but for me it is pointless. My number one goal when making films is to learn new techniques and improve my animation abilities."

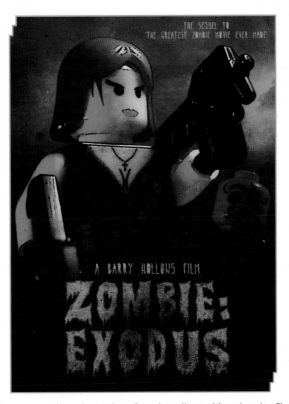

The promotional poster for Jonathan Vaughan's film *Zombie: Exodus.*
© Jonathan Vaughan

COMPETITIONS

Entering animation, stop-motion, and brick-film contests is a motivational and promotional tool that many of the animators in this book have used. Not only is it fun to create something for a particular purpose, but the competition rules set boundaries that can encourage creativity and speed the process along. "A competition can definitely give you something to focus on," said Chris Salt, who won a national radio contest with his film *Jane's Brain*. "You're usually given some kind of subject and a deadline, which narrows down your options and makes you think

Just some of the regular brick-filming competitions held over at Bricksinmotion.com.
© Philip Heinrich

more about what you can accomplish in the time available. Some people find that stimulates their imagination and some find it too restrictive."

If you're one of the latter, then Bricks in Motion's popular THAC event (Twenty-four Hour Animation Contest) might not be for you. The contest, which originated on Brickfilms.com and migrated to Bricks in Motion, has been held since 2005. Philip Heinrich, who runs the site, says "entrants must complete a film in a twenty-four-hour period of time. Despite the very short time span, this contest gets between seventy and one hundred entries every year."

Zach Macias is a serial contender for the THAC title. "I'm not even entirely sure of what keeps drawing me back to THAC year after year," he says. "I think what I like about it is that you have very little time to second-guess what you're doing. I often struggle with over-thinking my ideas to the point where I may abandon it entirely if I decide I don't like it anymore, but with THAC, if you want to hope to finish something in the timeline, you have to put all of those self-doubts aside and push on. They're not always the most polished films you'll ever make, but there does come a nice sense of accomplishment to conceptualize, write, shoot, and edit an entire short stop-motion film in a single day."

These contests are more about the experience, and winners usually receive modest prizes, but there can be additional benefits of doing well. Chris Salt said his public profile increased after winning and it led to offers of paid animation work. Competitions can usually be found on LEGO websites and forums and brick-film sites like bricksinmotion.com.

Entering a competition is a great way to kick-start a project and motivate yourself to finish, as well as restricting you to work within the parameters of the contest rules. It's also a great way to raise your profile and to get your work noticed, as Chris Salt discovered when he used LEGO stop-motion to win a national radio contest.

What kind of films do you make with LEGO, and how has your approach changed over time?

I generally make short films for my own amusement. That's been a constant throughout. Sometimes it'll be a silly joke and sometimes it'll be a song I like. The stop-motion side of things has changed very little since I started. The changes have been in other areas, especially in what's possible with digital postproduction. When I started out, I'd shoot the stop-motion footage, edit it together, and the film was done. Now that's just the first step. There's facial animation to add, color grading, masking, removing dust. . . . The list is endless, or seems so when I'm doing it.

Jane's Brain was made as your entry to a radio competition–LEGO stop-motion on the radio? Sounds interesting.

The Adam and Joe Show was a BBC Saturday morning radio show hosted by Adam Buxton and Joe Cornish. This particular show had a feature called Song Wars, in which each presenter would take a week to create a song with a specific theme and listeners would vote on which one they liked best. At some point they decided to involve the listeners a little more and set up the Video Wars competition. They chose two

Song Wars songs and asked people to make a video for one of them. I chose "Jane's Brain" because it was the shorter of the two.

The only real restriction was the song–how did you decide to interpret it?

Despite being a fan of the radio show, I'd missed the competition announcement and only found out about it three weeks from the deadline. That didn't leave a great deal of time for planning and preparation. The song's lyrics describe a woman in very simple terms—she

The title card for *Jane's Brain*.
© Chris Salt

© Chris Salt

has a brain, she likes cars, she goes shopping—so that formed the basis for the script/shot list. I just took everything absolutely literally and exaggerated it for comic effect.

The storyboards and set designs came together quite easily. It's a fast-paced song so I knew I could cut together lots of short shots in time with the music. I just had to decide what image would fit with each line. How do you illustrate a line that says, "She had a brain?" Put her in front of a blackboard. "She'd think of cars?" Show a bunch of cars. The silliness of the song really helped here.

With only three weeks to plan and produce the film, how did you juggle building your sets and finishing all the animation in time?

I spent a couple of weeks before the three-day shoot building cars, houses, and anything else I knew I was going to need. I already had a LEGO Cafe Corner set and there's another official LEGO set in the shot where Jane is thinking about the houses that she likes. The other sets, like the supermarket and the inside of Jane's house, were built as I was shooting. That's why they're comparatively simple. It was a case of building the bare minimum that would show up on screen.

A three-day weekend would normally be plenty of time to film a thirty second film but this one had a lot of scene changes and each shot had to be set up carefully so that transitions from one to the next would work. Because I'd spent some time planning and building sets in advance, production went surprisingly smoothly. I simplified some

The armature Chris created to make his car appear to drive through the hinged pieces of the billboard.
© Chris Salt

shots as I went along but the bulk of the film is exactly as I first envisioned it.

Was there anything you couldn't achieve that you would have liked to?

The main deviation from the storyboard came about because I had this crazy idea that I could drive a car through a supermarket window. I'd worked out how to do it, gumming individual 1 × 1 clear LEGO tiles to a sheet of clear plastic, then shooting frames of individual tiles and compositing them in to show the glass shattering and flying out. I still think it could look pretty cool but it would have taken weeks to shoot and fix up in postproduction. Instead, I went for the slightly easier shot of a car flying through a billboard. I didn't have time to set it up and film it during the weekend

shoot so I had to fit it in to the evenings of the following week. I finished the whole thing with about a day to spare before the competition deadline.

How did you create that awesome billboard shot?

It took some planning to set up and involved a lot of digital manipulation after the fact. I got so many questions about it that I actually put together a short video to show what was involved. Basically, I shot a blank billboard made up of hinged plates that could be pushed outward. I then pushed the car through it on the end of a big armature, gradually opening out the hinged sections as I went. With that footage in the can, I had to go through each frame in Photoshop, erasing things that shouldn't be there and adding the billboard poster.

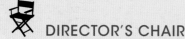

The finished sequence with the armature removed in postproduction.
© Chris Salt

What are the other visual effects in the film and how did you create them?

Aside from the billboard shot, the visual effects in *Jane's Brain* were quite simple. I wanted to add the supermarket sign to the front of the store and put some branding on the drinks machine. I could have edited each frame by hand but there wasn't a lot of time. I was careful to keep the camera still during the shot so that I could just draw them in Photoshop and superimpose them in my editing software.

Jane's Brain also contains my first experiment with face animation. I did it in much the same way I did the signs—again, I kept Jane's head still and used Photoshop to erase the printed mouth, then superimposed a series of hand-drawn "chewing" mouths.

The visual effect component has grown over the years. Where I used to be happy with regular minifigs and their printed faces, I now tend to shoot all the stop-motion footage with blank heads and then use After Effects to add in digitally animated faces afterwards. This more or less doubles the time it takes to finish a project.

Your hard work paid off, because you won the competition. What was that like?

It was a real surprise. I'd seen some of the other entries and several of them were really good. I thought I was maybe in with a chance of an honorable mention. I got to visit the radio station and meet the guys, and I appeared on the show a couple of times. The film appeared on the BBC website and I think Adam played it at one or two of his live shows.

You've worked with Adam Buxton on other videos since. What's that been like?

It's been fun. I came to *The Adam and Joe Show* as a fan so it's been great to stay in touch and work on new things. There's generally not a lot of collaboration involved. Adam creates a lot of audio skits and songs in his radio work and it's these that I animate. He's generally happy to just point me in the direction of a piece of audio and let me get on with it.

Jane's Brain was shot using a Panasonic camcorder and edited using Stop Motion Pro and Sony Vegas. To watch it and Chris Salt's other films go to www.youtube.com/user /0ldScratch and www.youtube. com/user/hurtinator for Chris's behind-the-scenes videos.

THE COMMUNITY

Bricks in Motion's Philip Heinrich says that it was the release of LEGO Studios in 2000 that helped to popularize the hobby in a big way online. But this was still half a decade before YouTube launched in 2005. "It was certainly not as easy in the pre-YouTube days," he says. "We uploaded our films to various webhosting and file hosting services, then shared them on community web forums. RealPlayer was king in early 2000s Internet video." With the launch of YouTube, brick-filmmakers from around the world were finally able to easily share their work

Bricks in Motion is a great place to watch the latest brick-films, find useful resources, and read about fun animation contests.
© Philip Heinrich

with a wider audience. "Originally, producing and putting an independently-made film online was actually a pretty involved process," says brick-filmmaker Zach Macias. "Now, anyone with access to the Internet has the ability to put their videos out there, which has opened the door for a lot of new animators otherwise unable to publish their works to easily do so."

For some members of the community, however, websites like brickfilms.com and then later bricksinmotion.com provided a place where animators could not only share their work but help each other to improve their stop-motion skills. "YouTube is a great place to post work and have it be seen, but it doesn't allow for the kind of discourse you can have in a community of regular members who share a serious common interest," Philip says. "We also have contests and other ongoing animation challenges to help people grow in skill and share their work with each other." But he admits there is less of a demand for the community site nowadays. "Only people interested in serious critique and discussions go to niche filmmaking community websites. That's not necessarily a bad thing for those of us who fit into that category."

Bricks in Motion, which was originally created by Jonathan Schlaepfer in 2007 and has been run by Heinrich since 2009, is the only English-language forum devoted to LEGO movies that has a consistent base of members. Heinrich says there are some other great communities such as Brickboard.de, EuroBricks, and The Brickfilmers' Guild. The Brickfilmers' Guild is a kind of social network for brick-filmmakers that works in tandem with the Bricks in Motion community. Bricks in Motion has superseded Brickfilms.com, which was a popular online community for many years, as Zach Macias remembers. "I joined the Brickfilms.com online forum back in early 2005, and I consider that the real inception of my career as a 'brick-filmer.' In its heyday, Brickfilms.com was like a haven, filled with a number of experienced, dedicated members passionate about not only helping out the newcomers, but actively trying to innovate and push the hobby forward, including the input of some actual professional animators." Zach explains that in the years since much of that community has migrated to Bricks in Motion, after the site was sold in 2007.

With websites like YouTube, Vimeo, and Daily-motion being so popular, brick-film sites are no longer necessary as a way for animators to promote their films, but Philip Heinrich says that Bricks in Motion offers something unique—"a community of like-minded storytellers who want to help each other improve. There is a level of discussion, analysis, and constructive criticism here that does not occur on video-sharing websites. The same is true, I believe, of many niche film-making websites." Indeed, there are many stories of users from the Bricks in Motion community who were inspired by the site specifically to take their hobby seriously, and in some cases pursue it as a career. "This is my prime motivation for keeping the community alive as best I can," says Philip. "I know I owe a great deal of my passion for filmmaking to this community, and it is a large part of what drove me to become an independent filmmaker."

Collaborating

For many, one of the joys of making stop-motion LEGO movies from home is that there's no need to involve anyone else. It's a hobby completely designed for flying solo and doing things your way. But for some, like Christian Colglazier, working with family for his films comes naturally. "I work with my brother for most of my films," he says. "He writes the scores for my films and gives me feedback on things I need to change. He also helps me a great deal in editing." But if the thought of team-building on your brick-film just doesn't compute, you're not alone. "I've never collaborated with someone in the sense of sitting down together and working on something as a team," says animator Chris Salt. "That's an approach that can be productive for some people but it doesn't really suit my way of working. If I get a new idea while I'm animating, I like to try it out and see how it looks. You can't really do that when you're working with others and they're expecting you to turn in certain scenes at certain times. There's an element of organization and project management required to see it through to completion."

But collaborating with others on your film isn't limited to co-directing/co-animating a film, as Chris has discovered. There are lots of other ways that your friends and family can be involved in your hobby. Other people bring great ideas, fresh insight, skills, and enthusiasm. Here are just some of the ways you can incorporate others into your projects.

- "I'm a member of a LEGO club in the UK called the Brickish Association," said Chris, "and through them I met and became friends with Peter Reid, who's very good at building things with LEGO. He's provided a lot of scenery and props for my films over the years and we're currently working together on designs for a short sci-fi adventure film." Borrowing LEGO and models from other builders is also a great way to improve the production values of your film at no extra cost.

- Sharing online sources and tips can help to develop your skills more quickly. If you're having trouble trying to create a particular effect, message other YouTubers who have been more successful and ask for their advice.

- Can't quite make your characters sound different enough or having trouble perfecting your Darth Vader impression? You'll be surprised by the voice talent just waiting to be discovered in your own house.

- Don't have all the equipment or LEGO to make your movie? Why not start a crowdfunding campaign online. Jonathan Vaughan did just this for his latest epic *Melting Point* (see the next page) and the reaction exceeded his expectations. Crowdfunding your film also helps to promote it prior to its release to get your audience excited.

- Want a unique soundtrack without having to pay licensing fees? Ask musician friends to strum guitars and create dance tracks to underpin key scenes in your films, or email local bands to see if you can use their tracks in your film for free.

- Making a movie in your bedroom can be tricky, especially if you've got wonky floors and big windows. If you don't have a suitable space to shoot your film, ask friends with unused garages or basements if you can borrow the space for your production. Who knows, you might even convert them to stop-motion too.

- When it comes to releasing your film, ask all your friends to share and like on social networking sites and view the film on YouTube to increase the film's online profile and get some viewer feedback.

- You might not want to make your film as a team, but banding together with other brick-filmmakers is a great way to organize contests, events, and screenings. Post on forums to find others in your area who want to get their film seen and approach your local movie theater about putting on an event.

The poster for *Melting Point*—this brick-film's budget came from crowdfunding website Kickstarter.
© Jonathan Vaughan

Find the funding

Playing around with LEGO stop-motion is not going to cost a fortune, but if you have a more elaborate film project in mind, you might find your LEGO collection, lighting set up, or studio space severely lacking. Crowdfunding websites are a great way to promote the film, build a following, and most importantly find the cash to make your film a reality. Rather than spending your own money, the involvement of others will give you the added motivation you need to see the project through to completion. Come up with unique rewards or perks you can offer your backers—having a LEGO minifigure based on them featured in the movie, letting them voice one of your characters, giving them a producer credit on the poster, or sending them a prop or set from the film are just some of the ways you can encourage people to pledge.

For his most recent film, *Melting Point*, Jonathan Vaughan turned to crowdfunding website Kickstarter to help with the financial costs of producing the film he had planned. The overwhelming show of support was a huge surprise. "*Melting Point* is the first film I've made that has a budget," he says. "None of my other brick-films have required any kind of financing, but the scale of *Melting Point* is so far beyond anything I've done before, and given my dislike for CGI I wanted to do everything in camera that I could. This necessitated the Kickstarter campaign." Jonathan had no idea what to expect, and despite having a decent following on YouTube he knew that wouldn't be enough to make the campaign a success. "I was completely blown away by what happened," he says. "My project was staff picked on Kickstarter, and over seventy percent of the pledges ended up coming from people who found the project while browsing, most of whom had never seen any of my work before. It was incredibly motivating to receive that kind of support, and gave me a lot more confidence about the whole project."

Swedish directors Daniel Larsson and Tomas Redigh are musical duo Ninja Moped (also known as Rymdreglage). They use stop-motion to create hypnotic videos for their electronic music. Tomas talks about their experience animating with LEGO bricks, and their hugely popular video *8-Bit Trip*.

© Daniel Larsson and Tomas Redigh

Was the video for *8-Bit Trip* your first foray into stop-motion with LEGO bricks?

No, my first LEGO stop-motion was called *Legoman*. It was a more regular LEGO stop-motion about the super hero Legoman who must save the son of the president who has been kidnapped. That video was used as a portfolio to help me enter film school in 2001.

It seems LEGO and your music were made for each other—did the *8-Bit Trip* music inspire the LEGO video or vice versa?

We took the photos first and then we made the song and cut the scenes to the music.

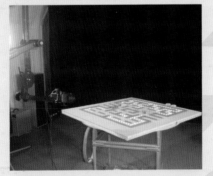

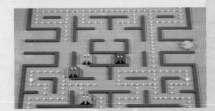

LEGO interpretations of classic games such as Pac-Man are incorporated into the video.
© Daniel Larsson and Tomas Redigh

8-bit video games came along when LEGO was rapidly expanding as a brand—was it this eighties nostalgia that you were trying to capture when you wrote the song? What are your early memories of LEGO?

Yes! LEGO and 8-bit games are very nostalgic for me. I remember the LEGO commercials—it was always a landscape with moon sand and LEGO space ships. Me and my brother always built crazy stuff with LEGO, like cannons with rubber bands to shoot LEGO bricks.

How much of the video was planned in advance?

All the scenes were created as small experiments so nothing was storyboarded.

Approximately how many LEGO bricks were used in the making of the video?

I bought new LEGO for the video because I didn't have many clean bricks—the ones I had were thirty years old. And I think we used about 30,000 bricks but we have a lot more now and will be using 160,000 bricks for our next video.

Where was the video shot?

I made a studio in an old barn at my parents' place with no heating, so some of the shooting took place in five degrees Celsius. It took about 1,500 hours to shoot over an eight-month period.

What was it like to have your body covered in LEGO bricks?

Both of us were covered and it was painful—after one hour it was like the small studs were penetrating into the skull. Almost. . . .

Which part of the video was the hardest to produce?

The part with two thumbs hitting the NES-controller. It took a lot of time every frame and my own thumbs were bleeding when I tried to remove the LEGO bricks from the board.

How did you feel about the video when it was finished?

I was extremely happy with it because I thought it had great potential, and the fact that I didn't have to work on it no more.

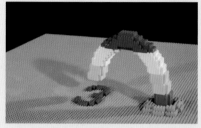

Thousands of bricks were used to build all the parts required to create the clever stop-motion effects.
© Daniel Larsson and Tomas Redigh

LEGO ninjas in a variety of positions, and in place in the finished film.
© Daniel Larsson and Tomas Redigh

Are you surprised by the millions of views the video has already received on YouTube? Why do you think people enjoy the video so much?

When we uploaded it we were totally unknown, so when we got two million views in a week it was a really strange feeling. A lot of newspapers all over the world wanted to interview us. Now we are used to it because it was years ago that we uploaded it. On the Internet I think people enjoy video-game stuff where lots of effort has gone into it.

If you were to produce the film again would you make any changes or do anything differently?

When we shoot the video for *8-Bit Trip 2*, we are going to do

Both band members committed themselves fully to the stop-motion process, covering their whole bodies in LEGO bricks!
© Daniel Larsson and Tomas Redigh

tripod or something so the surface is smooth, and have patience!

If someone wanted to appear in their own films, what is your advice for being a stop-motion actor?

Think about how you can do it with breaks so you don't have to stand still for eight hours.

***8-Bit Trip* was shot using a Nikon D90 with a standard 18–55mm lens and a Tamron 180mm macro lens. To watch the video and cool behind the scenes clips from the band go to www.youtube.com/user/ Ninjamoped and visit their website www.rymdreglage.se.**

a lot more cool camera-flys. Right now we are building the controller to move the camera wherever we want in the room. But for the first one, no, I think it is good as it is.

Do you have any tips or advice for other filmmakers looking to try stop-motion using LEGO?

Yes, use a high frame rate, use lighting that doesn't flicker, use a

USEFUL WEBSITES AND RESOURCES

Software

Below are links to all of the different computer programs mentioned in the book, where you can find free trials, downloads, and further instructions for how to edit and create visual effects.

Stop-motion animation

AnimatorHD: www.animatorhd.com

Dragonframe: www.dragonframe.com

FramebyFrame: www.framebyframe.en.softonic.com

iStopMotion: www.istopmotion.com

Monkey Jam: www.monkeyjam.org

Stop Motion Pro: www.stopmotionpro.com

The Helium Frog Animator: www.heliumfrog.com

Editing

Adobe Premiere Pro: www.creative.adobe.com/products/premiere

Final Cut Express: www.apple.com/support/finalcutexpress/

Final Cut Pro: www.apple.com/support/finalcutpro/

iMovie: www.apple.com/mac/imovie/

Sony Vegas: www.sonycreativesoftware.com/vegassoftware

Windows Movie Maker: www.windows.microsoft.com

Effects

Action Essentials 2: www.videocopilot.net

Adobe After Effects: www.creative.adobe.com/products/aftereffects

Adobe Photoshop: www.creative.adobe.com/products/photoshop

GIMP: www.getgimp.com

HitFilm 2 Ultimate: www.hitfilm.com
Pinnacle Studio: www.pinnaclesys.com
Sqirlz: www.xiberpix.net
Wax 2.0: www.debugmode.com/wax

Audio
Audacity: www.audacity.sourceforge.net
AudioMicro: www.audiomicro.com
Blue Yeti microphone: www.bluemic.com/yeti
Free SFX: www.freesfx.co.uk
Free Sound: www.freesound.org
Kevin MacLeod royalty-free music: www.incompetech.com
Machinima Sound: www.machinimasound.com
Pro Tools: www.avid.com
Soundsnap: www.soundsnap.com

Lighting
Dedolight: www.dedolight.com
Lifelites Micro Lighting Products: www.lifelites.com

Script writing
Celtx: www.celtx.com
Final Draft: www.finaldraft.com
Movie Magic Screenwriter: www.screenplay.com
Page 2 Stage: www.page2stage.com

Storyboard template
Printable Paper: www.printablepaper.net

Further reading and resources
Bricks in Motion: www.bricksinmotion.com
Eadweard Muybridge: www.eadweardmuybridge.co.uk
Stop Motion Central: www.stopmotioncentral.com
Doug Vandegrift's tutorials: www.youtube.com/user/cannedgravy
Video Copilot: www.videocopilot.net
Brick Trick (in German): www.bricktrick.de

ACKNOWLEDGMENTS AND CREDITS

Thank you to the wonderfully creative and dedicated animators who have contributed their tips, tricks, and photographs to this book. Special thanks go to Tony Mines for his expertise and insight and to Paul Hollingsworth for his photography. Paul would also like to thank David Kelly, Chris Osborn, Brent McDonald, Steve Banta, Ryan Jennings, Ray Silva, Amanda Hollingsworth, Voodoo Highway Music and Post.

Listed below are all of the animators whose work has been referenced in *Brick Flicks* and links to their YouTube pages or websites.

Adam Radwell: www.youtube.com/user/demondoggz
Chris Salt: www.youtube.com/user/0ldScratch and www.youtube.com/user/hurtinator
Christian Colglazier: www.youtube.com/user/Disney365Stitch
Daniel Larsson and **Tomas Redigh:** www.youtube.com/user/Ninjamoped and www.rymdreglage.se
Daniel Utecht: www.youtube.com/user/FilmsByDan
David Boddy: www.youtube.com/user/pe668
Jonathan Vaughan: www.youtube.com/user/NickDurron
Jordan Johnson: www.youtube.com/user/xxxfancypantsxxx
Keshen8: www.youtube.com/user/Keshen8
Kevin Sarp: www.youtube.com/user/Thorn2200
Lars Hassing: www.youtube.com/user/larschassing
Lindsay Fleay: www.rakrent.com
Martin Pullen
Michel Gondry: www.michelgondry.com
Paul Hollingsworth: www.digitalwizards.tv
Philip Heinrich: www.youtube.com/user/SmeagolStudios
Tony Mines: www.spiteyourface.com/
Zach Boivin: www.youtube.com/user/ZachFBStudios
Zach Macias: www.youtube.com/user/ZachMG

INDEX